Lane County

Pictorial Research by Gwen Thomsen
"Partners in Progress" by Dianne Donovan

Sponsored by the Lane County
Historical Society
Windsor Publications, Inc.,
Northridge, California

Lane County

An Illustrated History of the Emerald Empire

Dorothy Velasco

Windsor Publications, Inc.—History Book Division

Publisher: John M. Phillips
Editorial Director: Teri Davis Greenberg
Design Director: Alexander D'Anca

Staff for *Lane County: An Illustrated History of the Emerald Empire*
Senior Editor: Karl Stull
Assistant Editors: Marilyn Horn, Gail Koffman, Jerry Mosher
Director, Corporate Biographies: Karen Story
Assistant Director, Corporate Biographies: Phyllis Gray
Editor, Corporate Biographies: Judith Hunter
Editorial Assistants: Kathy M. Brown, Patricia Cobb, Lonnie Pham
    Pat Pittman, Deena Tucker, Sharon L. Volz

Designer: Christina McKibbin

Library of Congress Cataloging in Publication Data
Velasco, Dorothy, 1944-
    Lane County.

    Bibliography: p. 163
    Includes Index.
    1. Lane County (Or.)—History. 2. Lane County (Or.) —Description and travel. 3. Lane County (Or.)— Industries. I. Donovan, Dianne. Partners in progress. II. Lane County Historical Society (Or.) III. Title.
F882.L2V45   1985   979.5'3104   85-16864
ISBN 0-89781-140-2

Title page: *Pengra Bridge, depicted in watercolor by Carolyn Nuessle-Orum, was built in 1938. Its 126-foot lower chords are the largest ever cut from timber for an Oregon bridge. Courtesy, Lane County Fair Board*

CONTENTS

*To Hallie Hills Huntington, for
tirelessly preserving our local
heritage, and to the people of
Lane County, whose appreciation
of that heritage will serve as a
guide to the future.*

FOREWORD

Lane County, Oregon, is a remarkable place. It is one of only two counties on the Pacific Coast that stretch all the way from the sea to the Cascade-Sierra mountain crest. (Oregon's Douglas County is the other.) Lane County's 4,620 square miles are more than double the geographical extent of the state of Delaware. Its great natural beauty ranges from the spectacular Oregon coast to the glowing snow-capped peaks of the Three Sisters. In between is the lush Willamette Valley, flanked on both sides by towering forests of Douglas fir.

The climate is favorable, with average annual temperatures in the valley that vary from a mild 28 degrees in January to a pleasant 66 degrees in July. The winters are moist—the rains (and deep snow in the Cascades) produce an average annual precipitation of 46 inches—while the summers are like California at its best, with day after day of bright, sunny skies and low humidity.

The bustling Eugene-Springfield metropolitan area provides the urban center of Lane County and is the largest between Portland and Sacramento. Counterpointing the urban area are the neighborly small towns and villages from one end of the county to the other. Prosperous, well kept farms dot the valley floor; cabins nestle in the woods of the Coast Range and the Cascades; and wind-raked cottages confront the surging Pacific.

In the work place, Lane Countians find sustenance in the core industry of lumber, in the bounty of agriculture, and in the linked endeavors of business, the professions, commerce, and finance. Transportation, tourism, fishing, and recreation all contribute to the economic well being of the county. Headed by the nationally eminent University of Oregon, the county's excellent educational system affords a cultural base for the good life. Lane County takes pride in its highly acclaimed community college and presidentially commended secondary schools.

Few people on earth have been more blessed with comfortable and satisfying lives than have the residents of Lane County since its organization in 1851. Yet there have been periods of economic depression, and one of these has been under way since 1979 as national economic policy and conditions have produced widespread unemployment and business failure locally. In such times a sense of historical identity is all the more precious.

America's first great age of local history was in the late nineteenth century, when a pioneer generation turned to the assessment of its frontier past through the publication of hundreds of county histories in the Midwest and West. A representative example from this Golden Age of local history was Albert G. Walling's beautifully illustrated volume on Lane County, published in 1884. Since then, unfortunately, relatively little has been published on the subject. A particularly glaring omission until now has been the lack of a modern general history of the county. It is almost as if Lane Countians had been too busy.

The current economic hard times in Lane County have undermined efforts to preserve the heritage of our community. The Lane County Historical Museum is the center of local historical research and is a true community organization that serves all those interested in Lane County history from schoolchildren to scholars. As a publicly funded institution it has, however, suffered a drastic curtailment in staff with a resulting severe reduction in service. It may take a generation for Lane County to recover from these fiscal blows to the maintenance of its heritage.

Yet community interest in Lane County history remains high and, despite economic stringency, is rising rather than declining. The county has an active historical society, which since 1956 has published a valuable journal, the *Lane County Historian.* The interest in Lane County history is part of a national revival of interest in local history that began in the 1960s. Academic historians have come to realize that the national perspective can only be fully understood on the basis of a deep knowledge of communities, and nowadays some of the best books by university historians are written in the once-neglected field of local history. The revival has been especially vibrant at the grass-roots level. Families long established in their community have turned to local history to trace and affirm their roots, while newcomers have found it an engrossing way of attaching themselves to their new community. The increasing numbers of historically oriented Lane Countians fall into both categories, and all will find satisfaction in this long-overdue history of Lane County.

With careful, discriminating research, Dorothy Velasco has produced for the general reader an accurate and perceptive account that the scholar will also find interesting and useful. It is comprehensive and well balanced in its treatment of the most significant recent events as well as the traditional history of the pioneers.

Having gone from a population of 150 settlers in 1850 to 125,776 in 1950, and having more than doubled its population (to 270,650) in a brief thirty-year period (1950-1980), Lane County has a history of growth, change, and variety. These themes are abundantly demonstrated in this volume, which traces the story of Lane County from the pre-1840 era of the Indians to the contemporary time of the Valley River Center, the Eugene Downtown Mall, and the Hult Center for the Performing Arts. The basic economic and social trends are well chronicled, but the personal dimension is always in view as we read, for example, of the ordeal of the Lost Wagon Train of 1853, the entrepreneurship of timberman James Isaac Jones, and the intriguing colorful lives of Opal Whiteley and Joaquin Miller. These and many more examples of growth, change, and variety are all to be found in the pages of Dorothy Velasco's absorbing cavalcade of Lane County history.

Richard Maxwell Brown
Beekman Professor of
Northwest and Pacific History
University of Oregon

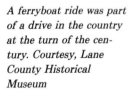

A ferryboat ride was part of a drive in the country at the turn of the century. Courtesy, Lane County Historical Museum

ACKNOWLEDGMENTS

This book could almost be considered to have a co-author in the person of Dr. Richard M. Brown, Beekman Professor of Northwest and Pacific History at the University of Oregon. Dr. Brown graciously consented to serve as consultant for the book, and his careful examination of the themes and facts presented in each chapter made an invaluable contribution to the project. His participation reflects a true love of local history and a desire to make that history available to the general reader.

Many other people were eager to see this book completed, and their generous help is evident throughout its pages. Hallie Huntington, president of the Lane County Historical Society, was an ardent supporter, as was Marty West, librarian for the Lane County Historical Museum, who always cheerfully hauled out files bulging with unexpected treasures.

Helpful information was provided about various organizations and events by the following contributors: Sally Sharrard, Springfield Planning Department; Bruce Hall, Pacific Northwest Bell; Gail Burwell, U.S. Forest Service; Bennie Youngren, Lane County Labor Council; Carolyn Kortge, *Register-Guard;* Ken Tollenaar, Bureau of Government Research; Kathy Jensen, Springfield Museum; Carol Daly, Lane County Historical Museum; Keli Osborn, Lane Community College; Tim Clodjeaux, University of Oregon Athletic Department; Richard Paulin, University of Oregon Art Muse-um; and Joyce Nichols, Weyerhaeuser Corporation.

Individuals who shared their special knowledge of events and persons include: Dr. Gerald W. Williams, Catherine Williams, Veryl Worth, Dr. Edwin R. Bingham, Alan Boye, Lawrence Hills, and Edna Temple. Institutional contributors include Sacred Heart Hospital, McKenzie-Willamette Hospital, Eugene Clinic, Northwest Christian College, Eugene Bible College, and the Eugene Area Chamber of Commerce. Thanks are due also to Dave Ramstead and Lois Barton of the Lane County Historical Society for their close readings of the manuscript.

Gwen Thomsen, photo researcher, gratefully received assistance in compiling photographs and illustrations from: Dr. Keith Richard, University of Oregon Archives; Martha Frankel and Marty West, Lane County Historical Museum; Nancy Kopeitka, Department of Economic Development, State of Oregon; George Rhoads, photographer; Don Hunter, photographer; Patricia Krier, University of Oregon Museum of Natural History; Rick Vaughn, Dot Dotson's Photo Finishing; Nancy Cutler, Lane Community College; James Hanson, Eugene Opera; John Lynch, Northwestern Photographics; Betsy Ford, Graphics Unlimited; Carolyn Nuessle-Orum, artist; Steve McCulloch, Lane County Fairboard. Judith Manning provided editorial assistance with the photo captions.

Borrowing A Living From The Land

A young Siuslaw Indian girl, standing ankle deep in muddy sand while digging clams, may have paused for a moment and looked out to sea. She may have seen a vision, something riding far out on the ocean close to the horizon, something with white billowing wings. And behind it, another. The girl—let us call her Yellow Bird—couldn't know how her life in a small village at the mouth of the Siuslaw River would be affected by that vision: two ships captained by James Cook, sailing north along the Oregon coast.

Yellow Bird could ask the shaman for an explanation, but for now she needed to hurry home with her clams. Home was a comfortable plank house with the interior excavated several feet below ground. The smell of smoke from the central fire pit mingled with dried fish hung from the beams of the pitched roof. It was fairly snug against the rain that fell during two-thirds of the year. If the weather got too wet and chilly,

The conical hat worn by Indian women of the Northwest tribes was watertight to protect against winter rains. Cold-weather clothing also included moccasins, leggings, and a cape of shredded cedar bark. Courtesy, Oregon Historical Society (neg. no. 49862)

Salmon was eaten fresh in season or dried or smoked to provide food throughout the winter. Courtesy, Oregon Historical Society (neg. no. 67537)

The canoe and basket were fundamental to an ancient way of life; yet this Northwest Indian woman doubtless watched her world change irrevocably as the nineteenth century came to an end. Courtesy, Oregon Historical Society (neg. no. 21058)

Yellow Bird put on a cape of shredded cedar bark, very much like her skirt. She could wear an intricately decorated conical hat, actually a watertight basket. She had moccasins and leggings for winter but needed little else in the way of clothing. Her ancestors had lived on the central Oregon coast for at least 5,000 years.

Yellow Bird knew little about the villagers who lived farther up and down the coast and who spoke different languages. Travel to the north was difficult because of high rocky headlands. To the south the endless-seeming sand dunes made a journey on foot exhausting. The ocean to the west was rough and cold, and the Siuslaw villagers rarely ventured into its waters in their cedar canoes.

The canoes were built to travel east, up the twisting Siuslaw River to the great inland valley. Near Yellow Bird's village, also to the east, was the Coast Range, with its rich timberlands and abundant wildlife. Here the men hunted bear, elk,

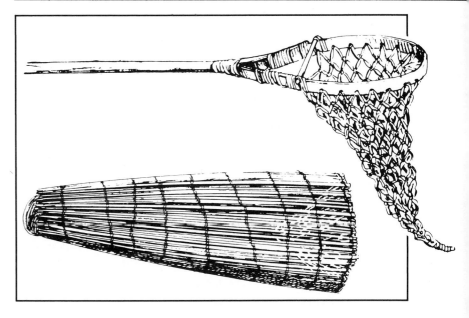

deer, cougar, and a variety of furbearing animals. Here they cut the great cedar logs, to be hollowed for their finely crafted canoes or split into planks for their houses. Here the women picked blackberries, wild strawberries, and other fruit.

Though it could take life if the people weren't careful, the ocean also gave life, in the form of fish, crab, clams, mussels, sea lions, and occasionally a whale run aground. Waterfowl offered a different type of meat as well as eggs. The river, too, provided food: the Siuslaw was a spawning stream for chinook and silver salmon and steelhead and searun cutthroat trout. Salmon was eaten fresh in season and either dried in the sun or smoked to last through the winter. The Siuslaw diet, seasoned with wild herbs, was varied and healthful. However, food supplies were often stretched to the limit by springtime.

One food staple not available on the coast was the camas root, a starchy bulb resembling a small onion. The camas grew inland, and to gather it during the summer Yellow Bird's family traveled with other families by canoe up the Siuslaw River to its headwaters in the long valley, now known as the Willamette. Situated between the Coast Range and the high Cascade Mountains, approximately 100 miles long and 20 to 30 miles wide, the large valley was divided into smaller valleys by clusters of rounded hills. The

trees on the hills, huge spreading oaks, weren't like the trees on the coast, and the lowlands were covered with high prairie grass.

The valley was divided also by numerous rivers. There was the majestic Willamette, with its Coast Fork and Middle Fork, as they would later be named. The slow-moving Long Tom and the brisk cold McKenzie flowed into the Willamette, which emptied into the Columbia River at present-day Portland. Numerous

Top left: *While some coastal Indian families used mats to roof their huts, planks were the most desirable covering. Courtesy, Oregon Historical Society (neg. no. 45809)* Above: *Weirs built of log, rock, or brush channeled fish into basket traps or into a shallow pond where they could easily be caught. Courtesy, Hilary Stewart*

streams traced their way through the rich soil to join the massive northward flow.

Indians had lived in this rich valley for at least 10,000 years, possibly much longer. It was a different land, with different people, the Kalapuyas. Although they spoke a language unintelligible to the Siuslaws, the two tribes could communicate using a simplified version of the Chinook language; this jargon later included adaptations of many English and French words.

The Kalapuyas generally allowed the Siuslaws to forage in their valley. After digging the camas roots out of the ground with a hardwood stick, the Indians roasted them for two or three days in pit-ovens. This staple more than any other kept the Kalapuyas alive through the winter.

Unlike the fish-dependent Siuslaws, the Kalapuyas relied mainly on vegetable foods such as roots, berries, nuts, and seeds. They included ground insects in their diet as well as large game. To facilitate hunting, the Kalapuyas would set fire to the prairie grass, forcing the game to flee to a certain area. Afterward the women gathered up the grasshoppers roasted in the fire.

Because they foraged for food, the Kalapuyas were not restricted to living in a permanent village except during the winter, when they lived in bark-and-plank houses. Their villages could vary in size from 20 to 500 inhabitants. Only the old and infirm stayed in the villages during the warmer months of the year, when extended families traveled up and down the valley, setting up temporary shelters as needed. They traded with other tribes and sometimes engaged in minor skirmishes. Like most Northwest tribes they captured slaves when they could. Village and tribal leaders gained power through a combination of wealth, including slaves and other goods, and political acumen. Children didn't necessarily inherit high social position; they had to earn it.

One learning process that adolescents, both boys and girls, underwent in many tribes was the quest for a vision. This quest consisted of going to a sacred place, such as a mountain, where spirits would communicate with humans. The seeker went alone, bathed daily in a creek, fasted, and sang spirit songs for five days. With luck a vision of a guardian spirit would appear, usually an animal. Yellow Bird must have believed she had had such a vision when she saw Captain Cook's ships far out to sea.

A man or woman with strong spirit powers could act as a shaman—a healer and ceremonial leader. Even some slaves became shamans, gaining a respected position in the community. The shaman knew hundreds of stories about the creation of the world and about the spirits in rocks, streams, plants, and animals, some of them good, some malevolent.

During the winter, when food gathering was minimal, there was time for storytelling and ceremonials, time for the young people to hear the ancient tales and learn the moral in them. The most common myths about the creation of the world involved the trickster Coyote, who created a generous but less-than-perfect world populated by less-than-perfect people.

In the middle of summer occurred the most important social and economic event in the lives of the Northwest Indians, the trade fair. Thousands gathered at sites on the Columbia River near Celilo Falls and present-day The Dalles. Some commodities, after being traded several times, ended up as far away as Alaska, Southern California, or Missouri. Salmon and slaves were most highly prized.

Whale and seal bone, obsidian and other stones, buffalo and deer skins, and all types of foods were also traded. Dentalia, the valuable crescent-shaped shells used to decorate clothing and baskets, served as ceremonial wealth rather than cash. Sewn onto ceremonial buckskin

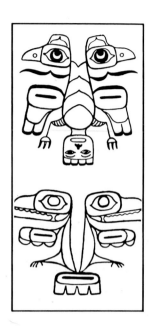

clothing, shells and feathers manifested opulence as plainly as a Rolls-Royce or a mink coat today, and for those who had marriage in mind, the trade fair was definitely the place to show off one's most ornate garments. Round dances and singing provided another reason to dress up in finest attire. Completing the entertainment for all were games, races, and the universally popular gambling, often a simple hand game with sticks.

Not all of the tribes went to the fairs. The Siuslaws did not, but through trading during other parts of the year they were undoubtedly affected by the exchange of goods and information. Yellow Bird and her people may have learned through the Kalapuyas that there were strange pale people far to the east. She couldn't know that she had already seen them quite close—in her vision of the white-winged sea monsters.

It was unlikely that Yellow Bird had much contact with the Molallas, a tribe living along the western slopes of the Cascade Mountains (a small number of

them still reside in Lane County). The Molallas spoke still another language and depended upon still another major source of food: big game. During the winter they stayed on the lower slopes of the mountains, but at other times they ranged the high altitudes in search of deer, elk, and bear. Like many Northwest tribes, the Molallas flattened the heads of some of their infants, creating a sloping forehead that was considered a sign of beauty. Among most tribes, tattooing on face and arms represented not only beauty but also social standing. It was also common to pierce earlobes and the nasal septum for wearing ornaments.

Northwest Indians, adorning themselves, their baskets and utensils, and their canoes and wood products, showed a high degree of artistic skill. This skill and other cultural achievements would develop no further during Yellow Bird's lifetime. On the contrary, a period of purgatory was soon to begin for the Indians.

When Captain Cook sailed his ships, the *Resolution* and *Discovery,* up the Oregon coast in 1778, he was by no means the first European to explore these waters, but it was he who discovered the enormous potential for Northwest trade. Over two centuries before Cook, both the British and Spanish had hoped to locate the mythical Strait of Anián, or Northwest Passage, connecting the Atlantic and Pacific oceans. If the strait existed, the long dangerous journey around Cape Horn could be avoided and an easy trade route to the Orient established. The Spanish explorer Bartólome Ferrelo may have sailed as far north as the coast of Oregon in 1542 before bad weather forced him to return south. In 1578-1579 Francis Drake may also have reached the Northwest, without finding the desired strait.

It wasn't until the eighteenth century that concerted exploration began. From Siberia, Vitus Bering mapped the southeast coast of Alaska in 1741; the Russians, who needed furs for clothing, began trading and hunting there in 1745. The Spanish, fearing encroachment by the Russians, renewed their interest in the Northwest. Bruno Heceta, Juan Perez, and Juan F. Bodega y Quadra all ventured up the Oregon coast in 1774 and 1775.

Three years later Captain Cook sighted a headland on a wet, blustery day; appropriately he named it Cape Foulweather. At Nootka Sound in present-day British Columbia his men traded buttons, tools, and metal utensils for furs at incredibly advantageous prices. Continuing to Macao, they discovered the furs could then

be sold to the Chinese for prices even more incredible.

In Great Britain word spread rapidly about the easy fortunes to be made, and a flood of trade ships began risking the lengthy voyage around the Cape, up the Pacific coast, across to China, and on around the world. An even greater number of ships ventured from Boston. Furs were the main attraction, but the quest for knowledge of the unknown region also drew botanists and other scientists. Between 1785 and 1820 at least 443 expeditions from eight or more countries reached the Northwest.

Considerable tension with Spain stimulated Great Britain to strengthen its claims in the region. George Vancouver was sent to make a definitive search for the Northwest Passage. After two years he would conclude that no such passage existed. In the first year of his exploration, like many before him, Vancouver unwittingly passed by the estuary of the Columbia River. Two weeks later, on

Meriwether Lewis and William Clark were commissioned by President Thomas Jefferson to explore the uncharted Northwest, as depicted by artist Dean Cornwell. Courtesy, Oregon Historical Society (neg. no. 4581)

Fort Vancouver, shown in an 1845 illustration, was the regional headquarters for the Hudson's Bay Company during the fur-trapping era in the Northwest. Courtesy, Oregon Historical Society (neg. no. 803)

May 12, 1792, the American Robert Gray, captain of the *Columbia,* entered the mouth of the river and named it for his ship. Gray passed the information on to Captain Vancouver, whose lieutenant then explored the river almost as far as the Willamette and claimed the area for Great Britain.

If the Northwest Passage couldn't be found by sea, some daring explorers thought they could find it by land. One such man was Alexander Mackenzie, sent by Canadian fur merchants to discover a water route to the Pacific. Mackenzie completed a phenomenal trek across the Canadian Rockies in 1793, the first man to cross the continent by land.

The United States purchased the Louisiana Territory from France in 1803, and the following year President Thomas Jefferson commissioned Meriwether Lewis and William Clark to lead a party of thirty in search of a trade route from the Missouri River to the Columbia. They were entrusted to map the land and collect scientific information. Their return to St. Louis in 1806 prompted an attempt, which proved unsuccessful, to build a fur-trading post on the Columbia. John Jacob Astor's Pacific Fur Company established a post at the mouth of the Columbia in 1811. Astoria became the first permanent Anglo-American settlement in the Northwest.

From Astoria, Pacific Fur Company trappers fanned out to discover the best trapping areas. In 1812 Donald MacKenzie and his party traveled the length of the Willamette Valley and named the McKenzie River (spelling was flexible in those days). The next year William Wallace and J.C. Halsey built a permanent post known as Wallace House near present-day Salem.

Because of pressure during the British-American War of 1812, the Astor company sold out in 1813 to the North West Company, a Canadian firm. In 1821 that company merged with the Hudson's Bay Company, which moved the regional headquarters 100 miles inland to Fort Vancouver. As chief factor (business manager), Dr. John McLoughlin became the most influential white man in the Oregon Country for many years. He introduced agriculture in the region, since it was company policy to develop self-sufficient posts, and even raised cattle, the first of which were brought to the post by ship.

By the time Fort Vancouver was established trappers had beaten out a good trail system based on Indian trails. One route followed the Long Tom River on the west side of the Willamette toward the southern end of the valley and then turned down to the Umpqua River. Another main trail, requiring more river crossings, went down the east side of the Willamette.

The Indians were apprehensive about these intrusions into their land but wholeheartedly welcomed the goods received in exchange for furs. Metal tools and cooking utensils—sometimes even a gun—made life easier. Beads and buttons beautified their garments. The white man's clothing was so greatly esteemed that by the time the first wagon trains came to Oregon the emigrants found that many of the Indians had adopted various degrees of "civilized dress."

Intermarriage was common between trappers and Indians and was encouraged by the Hudson's Bay Company. Generally trappers felt at home with the Indians. Dr. McLoughlin, a Scotsman, married the daughter of a chief. Eventually some trappers, many of them French Canadians, and their families turned to farming and settled French Prairie in northern Willamette Valley.

Relations between the Hudson's Bay Company and the Indians were remarkably peaceful. A great deal of credit goes to Dr. McLoughlin who, with few exceptions, treated the Indians wisely and humanely. It was company policy not to interfere with tribal affairs or to impose European culture upon the Indians.

Nevertheless the white man brought catastrophe to the Indians. Smallpox, measles, malaria, and other fatal diseases new to the area caused ravaging epidemics along the Oregon coast as early as 1782. Willamette Valley Indians were stricken during the early 1830s. By that time, as many as 75 to 90 percent of the Indians in western Oregon had perished. Entire villages and even tribes had disappeared by the time the first missionaries and settlers arrived. The survivors were ill-equipped to revive their traditional social structure. White settlers misunderstood the abject state of the Indians, grossly underestimating their previous level of culture.

The first missionary in Oregon, the Methodist Reverend Jason Lee, had little influence over the dwindling number of Indians, but his influence on future settlement was enormous. The towering young preacher came to the Oregon Country in 1834 with Nathaniel Wyeth's trade caravan. At Dr. McLoughlin's suggestion Lee, with his nephew Daniel and three laymen, selected a mission site just north of present-day Salem. There they built a log house and in the spring began farming.

Realizing he needed to attract missionaries with practical skills Lee requested that the Mission Board send farmers, blacksmiths, doctors, and carpenters, preferably married men with families. In a letter to a friend he wrote: "A greater favour could not be bestowed upon the country, than to send to it pious, industrious, intelligent females."

The Mission Board complied, sending a contingent of recruits by ship in 1837, including a bride for Lee. Anna Maria Pittman, a plain-featured but devoted schoolteacher, died in childbirth less than a year after their marriage. Lee learned of her death while traveling east to gain support for expanding the mission; he had no choice but to continue his journey. In Washington, D.C., Lee presented to Senator Lewis F. Linn of Missouri a petition stating that the United States should hasten to claim jurisdiction in Oregon. The petition eloquently described the agricultural potential, the commercial advantages, and the importance of future statehood. It was a direct plea for government action and for the large-scale immigration that soon followed.

While in the East, Lee married Lucy Thompson, who had recently graduated at the head of her seminary class. Upon reading a copy of her valedictory address, he is reported to have exclaimed, "I must know that lady!"

In 1839 the Lees set sail for Oregon on the *Lausanne,* along with more than fifty missionaries—the Great Reinforcement—who were to be dispatched to new missions throughout the Northwest, as far as Puget Sound. Most of the branch missions were not successful in converting the Indians; moreover, some of the missionaries had trouble adapting to the rough living conditions. They accused Lee of spending more time on secular affairs like building a sawmill and lobbying for immigration than on ministering to the Indians.

In spite of his many accomplishments, complaints by branch missionaries undermined Lee's position with the Mission Board and eventually led to his dismissal as superintendent. Adding to his grief, Lee's wife Lucy died shortly after childbirth. Although he was later exonerated by the church, he died in the East, a broken man at age forty-one.

Neither Lee nor his missionaries had as much influence over the Indians as had the Catholic priests, Father Francis Blanchet and Reverend Modeste Demers, who came to French Prairie in 1838.

Nevertheless, Lee's encouragement of American expansion to the Oregon Country was instrumental in determining the type and number of settlers who would soon swarm into the Willamette Valley.

Yellow Bird, by this time an ancient woman in her seventies, had watched most of her family die of disease after the arrival of the whites. Her village was impoverished and demoralized. Gazing out to sea, she often remembered her vision of long ago, the winged sea monsters, and wished she had never laid eyes on them.

By the turn of the century, few Indians remained who remembered the days of prosperity and health among the tribes. Courtesy, Oregon Historical Society (neg. no. 49385)

OREGON FEVER: THE SETTLERS ARRIVE

I t may be asked, why did such men peril everything—burning their ships behind them, exposing their helpless families to the possibilities of massacre and starvation, braving death— and for what purpose?

I am not quite certain that any rational answer will be given to that question.

—James Nesmith, diary, 1843

It is probably destiny to which account I place it, having neither time nor good reason to offer in defense of so wild an undertaking.

—Jesse Applegate, letter, 1843

So wrote two of Oregon's leading citizens. They may not have been able to explain why, but along with thousands of other hopeful seekers, they packed their entire families—sometimes three generations—into sturdy, well stocked wagons and gathered with other families at

 OREGON TRAIL
AS OF 1846
COMPILED FROM AUTHENTIC DATA
United States Department of Agriculture
Bureau of Public Roads
WASHINGTON, D.C.

The Oregon Trail—2,000 arduous miles long—led set-
tlers toward the Willamette Valley where there was rich
soil and a mild climate. The first wagon train to follow
this trail, comprising about seventy people, set out in
1841. By 1845 "Oregon fever" had raised the number of
emigrants to 3,000. Courtesy, Lane County Historical
Museum

Oregon-bound families, leaving Missouri in the spring, spent five to seven months on the trail before reaching their destination. Courtesy, Oregon Historical Society (neg. no. 46054)

St. Joseph or Independence, Missouri. In the springtime they said good-bye to the civilized world and headed west toward the edge of the continent.

The wagons journeyed across the 2,000-mile Oregon Trail in five to seven months, passing through Fort Kearney on the Platte, then Fort Laramie 300 miles farther along. It was 280 miles to South Pass over the Rockies, another 110 dusty miles to Fort Bridger, and 230 miles to Fort Hall on the Snake River. There the trail forked and a sign reading "to Oregon" pointed right. An arrow pointed left toward California. Oregon legend holds that those who could read took the right fork.

The next stop was Fort Boise, and then the last crossing of the Snake River, the Grande Ronde Valley, the Blue Mountains, and The Dalles on the Columbia, where the Indians had held their trade fairs. And finally they went down the Columbia on rafts or, after 1845, took the steep and rocky Barlow Road around Mt. Hood. It was the epic American migration, and most travelers who chose Oregon headed on to the land of their ex-

pectations, the lush Willamette Valley.

These were solid citizens from Illinois, Indiana, Ohio, Kentucky, Missouri—people who had recently settled those frontiers. Their heritage was English, Scottish, and Irish. Most were Protestants, most were conservative, and most of them wanted to improve their lives rather than make a radical change.

Although many of the emigrants didn't quite know why they caught the "Oregon fever," any of several strong motivations may have been at work. One was the economy. The Panic of 1837 caused food prices to drop, and many farmers were unable to pay their mortgages. However, those who traveled to Oregon were not among the poorest because equipment and supplies for the trip were costly. Another compelling reason was health. Malaria-type fevers, called "fever and ague," were epidemic in the river bottomlands of the Midwest. Smallpox and cholera were also common. People believed that the clean new Oregon Country would be free of such terrors. Generally this was true, although cholera and other diseases killed far more people in the wagon

ON THE OREGON TRAIL

A typical Oregon Trail diary, preserved at the Oregon State Historical Society, is that of Elizabeth Smith. Leaving Indiana in April 1847, the Smith family reached St. Joseph on June 3, rather a late start for their journey to the Willamette Valley.

June 3. No one should travel this road without medicine, for they are almost sure to have the summer complaint. Each family should have a box of physicing pills, a quart of castor oil, a quart of the best rum and a large vial of peppermint essence.

June 19. Made twenty miles. Every night when we encamp we make quite a village. . . . We have plenty of music with a flute and a violin and some dancing.

June 23. We see thousands of buffaloes and have to use their dung for fuel. . . . Three bushels will make a good fire. We call the stuff "buffalo chips."

July 8. Today we had the most dreadful hailstorm I ever witnessed, in which a young woman and I came near being caught as we went out to the famous Chimney Rock. . . . They say that about here it is subject to tornadoes.

August 1. Passed over the Rocky Mountains, the backbone of America. It is all rocks on top and they are all split up and turned edgeways. Oh, that I had time to describe this curious country.

August 12. Fort Bridger. Here we have a good time for washing, which we women deem a great privilege.

August 22. Soda Springs. . . . Not so good as represented. It tastes like vinegar with a little saleratus [baking soda] in it.

August 29. Sixteen miles. You in "the States" know nothing of dust. It will fly so that you can hardly see the horns of the tongue-yoke of oxen. . . . And then in our wagons, such a spectacle—bed, clothes, victuals and children all completely covered.

September 12. The Indians along the Snake River go naked except an old rag tied around their hips.

By this time people in the wagon train were dying. One woman lost her reason and set fire to a wagon. Supplies were short.

October 23. Camped on the Columbia River. Scarce feed. . . . We had to burn little green weeds.

The Smiths waited weeks for passage down the Columbia to Portland. The weather turned freezing. Then Elizabeth Smith's husband fell ill.

November 20. Rain all day. It is almost an impossibility to cook . . . . I froze or chilled my feet so that I cannot wear a shoe, so I have to go around in the cold water in my bare feet.

The Smiths landed in Portland on November 29 and moved into a leaky shed.

January 16. Portland has two white houses and one brick and three wood-colored frame buildings and a few log cabins.

February 2. Today we buried my earthly companion. Now I know what none but widows know: that is, how comfortless is a widow's life; especially when left in a strange land without money or friends, and [with] the care of seven children.

Mrs. Smith took up a homestead and later remarried. One of her sons became a judge and a stepson became governor.

The venturesome spirit of the early settlers was celebrated in the 1920s at the annual Pioneer Pageant. Shown here is Cal Young's replica of a covered wagon. Courtesy, Lane County Historical Museum

Beacon Rock marked the last leg of the Oregon Trail for emigrants who rode by flatboat down the Columbia River. Others completed their journey via the steep and rocky Barlow Road. Courtesy, Oregon Historical Society (neg. no. 5229)

trains than Indian arrows or bullets did.

The lure of adventure, of starting anew, of taming the wilderness and building new towns was undeniable for some, even among staid family men in their forties and fifties. Moreover, they could wear their Oregon fever as patriotism: missionaries, senators, and newspaper editors were exhorting nationalistic citizens to "go west" and settle the Oregon Country for the United States. The influx of settlers did strengthen the U.S. claim to the area, and in 1846 the boundary between British and American territory was fixed at the 49th parallel, the current border between Washington state and Canada.

The first settler to stake a claim in what became Lane County was Elijah Bristow, a fifty-eight-year-old grandfather and native of Virginia whose shock of white hair usually stood straight up. In June 1846, Bristow traveled through the Willamette Valley accompanied by Eugene F. Skinner, Felix Scott, and William Dodson, all of whom had crossed

the plains in 1845. In search of prime farmland they reached a point between the Coast and Middle forks of the Willamette River, where rolling meadows dotted with oak, fir, and pine must have struck some chord of recognition in Bristow's heart. It is widely reported that he declared: "This is my claim! Here I will live, and when I die, here shall I be buried."

Bristow named the spot Pleasant Hill and with his friends erected a small claim cabin of fir logs. After helping Bristow mark off a 640-acre claim of public-domain land, a square mile, Dodson and Scott marked off adjoining claims. Scott soon changed his mind and moved to the south bank of the McKenzie. Skinner went downriver some miles until he found a site at the foot of a low hill. Then called *Ya-po-ah* by the Indians, that hill has been known ever since as Skinner's Butte. Using Chinook jargon, a few Kalapuyas convinced Skinner to build his cabin on higher ground because of floods. The site of his first cabin is now the intersection of Lincoln and Second streets.

To this tiny log cabin Eugene Skinner brought his wife Mary and their infant daughter Mary Elizabeth in the spring of 1847. For several months Mary was the only white woman in the region that would become Lane County (Bristow's wife, bringing several of their fifteen children, couldn't make the journey from the East until 1848). Although they had already lost three daughters to illness back

in Illinois, the Skinners eventually raised several children born on the homestead.

Thin and dark-eyed, never in robust health, Skinner did not choose the best farmland for his claim. He had studied law and wasn't primarily a farmer. Evidently he intended to plat a town and sell the parcels to future residents. His claim did include a good site for a ferry crossing to the rich farmlands on the other side of the Willamette.

Settlers soon arrived to claim that land. The 1847 migration proceeded up the new Applegate Trail through southern Oregon. Taking the claim next to the Skinners' was Charnelton Mulligan, for whom Charnelton Street is named. Prior Blair settled nearby to the west; Blair Boulevard is named for him. Other close neighbors, some with families, included Wickliff Gonley, Benjamin Davis, John Akin, Jessie Gilbert, Lester Hulin, and

Eugene Skinner, for whom the city of Eugene was named, wasn't a farmer like most of the early settlers. His plan was to plat a town and sell parcels to future residents. Courtesy, Lane County Historical Museum

For a newly arrived couple, home was a rough-hewn cabin furnished with a few treasured belongings. This man and woman may not have been among the earliest settlers, but the unusual guitar must have been the first of its kind in Lane County. Courtesy, Lane County Historical Museum

H. Noble. A daughter was born to the Nobles in November of 1847, probably the first white child born in the county, although that honor is usually given to Leonora Skinner, born September 1, 1848.

Closer to Bristow's cabin in the Pleasant Hill area, new settlers included Cornelius Hills, Charles Martin, and Elias Briggs, who eventually founded Springfield. Between the two settlements A. Cargell and his bachelor son Louis took a claim. Arriving in 1848 were T.D. Hinton, Thomas Cady, David Chamberlain, Walter Montieth, and various branches of the Richardson, Vaughn, Hendricks, and Bristow families. Jacob Spores brought a canoe to the McKenzie River and began ferrying travelers across.

Willamette Valley homesteaders knew there was a war being fought against the Cayuse Indians around Fort Walla Walla, far to the northeast, but locally the Kalapuyas were generally friendly and never attacked. The only report of a white person's death at the hands of the Kala-

puyas dates back to the era of the Hudson's Bay trappers, when a young Englishman named Spencer went to hunt on a large butte called *Champ-a-te* (Rattlesnake Mountain). His companions found him dead and mutilated; they named the spot Spencer Butte. A later story attests that missionary Elijah White named it for President John Tyler's secretary of war.

The estimated population of Lane County for 1848 was 150, and it probably didn't increase the following year. It may even have dropped temporarily as men and boys hurried south for the California Gold Rush. They usually left their wives and younger children in charge of the Oregon homestead. Some wives became more prosperous than their prospector husbands by raising produce, which was sent by pack train to California and sold at vastly inflated prices. Women also made excellent profits by offering meals and lodging to the many travelers going to or returning from the gold fields. Although the Gold Rush slowed the settlement of Oregon, it stimulated rapid economic growth, both in agriculture and logging. The supply of lumber shipped from Portland to San Francisco could hardly keep up with the demand.

Eugene Skinner resisted the Gold Rush, and his home became a trading post of sorts. After Oregon was recognized by Congress as a U.S. Territory in 1849, Skinner's cabin became the local polling place and post office, receiving weekly mail from Salem.

Elias Briggs, too, dreamed of a town and prosperous enterprises, and in 1849 he moved from the Pleasant Hill area to a new claim three miles southeast of Skinner's, just across the Willamette. On low flat land next to a bubbling spring, he built his cabin, naming it Springfield.

Briggs immediately went into the ferrying business to serve travelers to the gold fields. He hired his neighbor William Stevens to operate the ferry, not

A replica of the Skinner cabin is located in Skinner's Butte Park in Eugene. Courtesy, George Rhoads

27

Hard-working and self-reliant, women did their part in the settlement of Lane County. During the California Gold Rush, many were left in charge of the homestead and some prospered by shipping farm produce south to market or by offering meals and lodging to traveling prospectors. Courtesy, Lane County Historical Museum

an easy job at first. Wagons and carts were dismantled and the pieces were placed on two canoes strapped together. Stock animals had to swim alongside the canoes across the wide cold river.

Once Oregon was a U.S. Territory, Congress passed the Donation Land Act in 1850 to formalize homesteading procedures and to encourage emigration. The act granted a white or part-Indian couple 640 acres of public land—320 acres for the husband and 320 acres for the wife in her own right—if they settled on or before December 1, 1850. For three years after that date half the amount of land would be granted.

An unforeseen result of the Land Act was a rush to marry any available female. The marriage of girls as young as ten or twelve was deplored by most residents, but there was no law against it. In many cases the child bride remained with her family until she was old enough to join her husband.

A few of these girls may even have been lucky enough to go to school. Lane County's first school, a small log cabin, was built in 1850 by Elijah Bristow, on his property in Pleasant Hill. His son William served as teacher; instruction was free and public. William later rose to prominence as a state senator.

The elder Bristow also organized the Pleasant Hill Christian Church in 1850, the first church of that denomination in the Oregon Territory and the first of any denomination in Lane County. W.L. Adams, a circuit rider, preached the first sermon to twenty-one charter members and performed the marriage ceremony of Johnson Basket and Katie Bristow.

In 1851 Lane County was created from Benton and Linn counties; the name derived from General Joseph Lane, first territorial governor of Oregon. Originally the county included all of southern Oregon (and presumably reached from the Pacific Ocean to the Rockies) but eventu-

Fall Creek School, shown in an 1887 photograph, was representative of early Lane County schools, in which one teacher taught all the grades. Courtesy, Dot Dotson's

William Bristow taught at the first school in Lane County and later rose to prominence as a state senator. The occasion of this photo remains unknown, though it may have been a wedding picture. Courtesy, Lane County Historical Museum

ally was cut down to its present size of 4,620 square miles.

The year 1851 opened a period of feverish activity in the Willamette Valley. There were cities to dream up and fortunes to make. In March the well-to-do Judge David M. Risdon hired Hilyard Shaw to build the first frame house in the future city of Eugene. Located on what is now Pearl Street, between Broadway and Tenth, this 14-by-20-foot structure was covered with split boards on the sides and roof. Shaw charged the judge a total of $76. He also dug a well and made pine furniture for the new house.

In April Eugene Skinner and Judge Risdon established a meridian line for surveying a town. The first survey was made in August and recorded the next year. The plot was located to the east of Skinner's Butte and extended as far south as Seventh Street. There were twenty-four blocks of eight lots each, and two fractional blocks. Skinner donated lots to James Huddleston for a store by Skinner's ferry landing and to Hilyard Shaw for mill construction. Mary Skinner was given the honor of officially naming the town, which she called Eugene City.

The new community soon gained the well deserved nickname of "Skinner's Mudhole," as the winter of 1851-1852 brought extensive flooding. Several cabins in Eugene and Springfield were destroyed. Though it was a hard way to learn, the receding waters of the floods did show the settlers the best sites for building millraces and mills, which were high on the agenda for development. To obtain flour the first homesteaders had traveled 100 miles to Oregon City, a ten-day round trip. By 1848 a flour mill had opened in Salem, and a closer one near Brownsville started up the following year. After the 1851-1852 floods enterprising settlers began building millraces and flour and woolen mills and sawmills in Eugene, Springfield, and the Pleasant Hill area. Hilyard Shaw and Avery Smith dug the millrace in Eugene.

Avery Smith and Hilyard Shaw built the Eugene Mill Company and dug the town's millrace. The portion of the building at the right is the original mill. Courtesy, Lane County Historical Museum

The County Clerk's Building, the fourth building constructed in Lane County, is preserved next to the Lane County Historical Museum. Courtesy, George Rhoads

Dr. A.W. Patterson, seated at the left in this family portrait, took an active part in the development of Eugene, as a surveyor, a physician, and later a state senator. Courtesy, Lane County Historical Museum

The Springfield millrace was built in 1852 by Isaac Briggs and his brother Elias, who borrowed a substantial amount of money from Jeremiah Driggs and Thomas Montieth, part-owners of an Albany mill. The Briggs sent to the East for an experienced millwright. Following the millwright's detailed scientific instructions, the Briggs brothers and T.J. Henderson, who later founded the First National Bank of Eugene, dug a lengthy canal using shovels and an ox-drawn plow, and built a log dam. Within a year the Briggs' newly constructed sawmill had made Elias and his brother two of the most prosperous residents of the county.

By 1852 the first session of the district court was held in Eugene City, with the Honorable O.C. Pratt on the bench. The bench—until a courthouse was built a few years later—was often located under an old oak tree. Lane County voters selected three county commissioners,

Blacksmithing was one of the earliest services required in the growing town. John Sloan's shop is shown here as it was in 1866 at Eighth and Olive in Eugene. Courtesy, Lane County Historical Museum

The Mahlon Harlow family opened their home on Sundays for Baptist services in the years before a church building was erected. Courtesy, Lane County Historical Museum

Joseph Davis, Aden G. McDowell, and Barnet Ramsey, who held their first meeting in Eugene City on September 6, 1852. There were forty citizens living in the town that year.

To stimulate development, Skinner donated several lots, two of which went to Matthew P. Deady and Ruben P. Boise, who became well known judges. Lots 5 and 8 in block 24 he donated as school sites.

Mahlon H. Harlow, for whom Harlow Road is named, established the First Baptist Church in his home, two and a half miles out of town. Years passed before the first church buildings were erected. Most worshipers eagerly awaited the periodic arrival of circuit riders of any denomination. One of the best known was Joab Powell, a huge man who had no formal education but had a booming voice, which many claimed could be heard a mile and a half away.

Since Eugene City consisted mainly of undeveloped lots, it was not to be taken for granted that the county seat would be within its boundaries. In 1853 Skinner, Charnelton Mulligan, Prior Blair, and a settler near Springfield offered land for county buildings; only Skinner's property was inside the platted town. Assured the town would grow, the county commissioners voted to accept forty acres from

Skinner and an adjoining forty acres from Mulligan. Appointed to survey the site was Dr. A.W. Patterson, a recent immigrant from Pennsylvania who later became involved in developing the public school system and served as a state senator. Prior Blair received $100 to construct the County Clerk's Building on the public square, the fourth building in Eugene. This 16-by-20-foot Greek Revival structure, one of the oldest public buildings still standing in Oregon, has been moved several times and is now preserved next to the Lane County Historical Museum at the Fairgrounds.

Eugene's first school was private, taught by Sarah Ann Moore in a log cabin on land known as "point of the hills," near present-day Twenty-fifth and University streets. Rattlesnakes, skunks, and owls often disrupted classes. Most private schools were short-term ventures, becoming less profitable after the public schools opened their doors.

By 1853 the need for improved transportation throughout the county and beyond was acutely evident. County road supervisors, appointed the previous year, ordered a road built from Jacob Spores' property via Skinner's ferry to intersect a north-south road along the Long Tom River.

Of even greater importance was the need for an Oregon Trail cutoff leading directly west to the Willamette Valley. Such a cutoff would eliminate 200 miles from the trip, avoiding the difficult passage down the Columbia by boat and the dangerous Barlow Road. Meetings were held in the homes of Elias Briggs and Mahlon Harlow to plan for the Free Emigrant Road, which in contrast with the Barlow Toll Road would attract many settlers, whose funds were often depleted by the last stretch of the journey. A series of exploration parties journeyed up the Middle Fork of the Willamette to find a pass through the Cascades; on one of these trips William Macy and John

Diamond climbed to the summit of a mountain that is now called Diamond Peak.

In the spring of 1853 Dr. Robert Alexander, in conjunction with his son James and with Jacob Spores, contracted to build a road through the Cascades to the west branch of the Deschutes River by June 15. They believed the distance was forty miles; it was really twice that, and by June a second contract granted an extension of time. Local residents donated a total of $2,463.50 toward building the road, a surprising amount of hard cash in those days of barter.

In July a thirty-five-year-old Kentuckian named Elijah Elliott set off from Lane County to meet his family on the Oregon Trail. He promised to spread word about the Free Emigrant Road and to lead a wagon train along the new route, even though he had never seen it. Thus began the often-told story of the Lost Wagon Train, which has stirred listeners for generations. Some local historians argue that the wagon train was never really lost. Lost or not, the travelers suffered tremendous hardships and probably would have perished if they hadn't been rescued from starvation and exposure by Lane County settlers.

Elliott joined his wife and children on the Oregon Trail, and in late August he began gathering a train for the Willamette Valley cutoff at the Malheur River, near present-day Vale, Oregon. On August 28 or 29 Elliott and about 100 men, women, and children in 20 wagons left the Oregon Trail, traveling west along the muddy Malheur. Within days nearly 100 wagons had taken the cutoff and caught up with Elliott. Eventually, as others continued to follow their tracks, more than 1,000 emigrants in 250 wagons were following a guide who knew little more than they did about the road ahead. Elliott retraced the route of Stephen Meeks, who had made an unsuccessful attempt in 1845 to lead a wagon train through the same area.

Many of the travelers came in large family groups. The McClure-Bond party had thirteen wagons. The Kinney family, John Kline, Tom Clark, James Watson, James Leonard, and Dr. Langley Hall all drove large herds of cattle with them on the new route, which soon proved to offer only scant grazing and water through many long stretches. John and Janet Stewart, originally of Scotland, took the cutoff with their four daughters, two of whom were married to Warners, family friends from Pennsylvania who were traveling in the same wagon train. The two younger Stewart daughters, seventeen-year-old Agnes, who later married yet another Warner, and her sister Helen, kept diaries along the trail. Agnes once bemoaned the rough travel: "Oh dear, if we were only in the Willamette Valley or wherever we are going, for I am tired of this."

They were all tired, and their animals were dying at an alarming rate. Elliott lost the travelers' confidence when he insisted on going north around Malheur Lake; the majority wanted to go south, which they did. When Elliott rejoined the group, there was some grumbling about lynching him, but Mrs. Elliott pleaded convincingly for his life.

Before the wagon train reached the mountains, food and potable water became equally scarce. At one point the McClure party had to return to a previous camp, where the bones of the cattle they had butchered for food three days before could be boiled for the marrow.

On September 14 an advance party set out on horseback to seek help. Benjamin Owen, Andrew McClure, Joe Denning, Charles Clark, Robert Tandy, Pleasant Noland, and James McFarland headed toward the Three Sisters, mistaking them for Diamond Peak. Instead of finding the Deschutes and the Middle Fork, they found the headwaters of the McKenzie. Sick and starving, eventually having to

eat their horses, they were not rescued until after the main group had been found and saved.

By October the wagon train finally reached the Deschutes, where they found road markers but nothing that resembled a wagon road. Apparently the road builders thought that marking the way was sufficient. The emigrants had to cut through thick forests on steep slopes for the wagons to inch forward.

The Thomas Williams family, originally of Wales, found some late mountain berries and opened their last barrel of sugar. But it wasn't sugar. The barrel contained rice, a brief feast for about fifty hungry people.

Martin Blanding, who had no family, decided to go ahead for help. He managed to get through to the small Willamette Valley settlement of Lowell in mid-October. Messengers rode through the valley all night calling for assistance; the fledgling communities responded with generosity. Settlers donated cattle to be slaughtered and hundreds of pounds of flour and staples. They rode up into the mountains, fed the emigrants, and guided them down to the valley, where many residents shared their homes with the newcomers until cabins could be built.

Eugene City's population—40 the year before—had jumped by the end of 1853 to 120. The population of Lane County undoubtedly increased by a comparable percentage. The influx of settlers brought many changes to the valley. Within a year a school district was formed, churches were chartered, and stagecoaches began running north and south along the Applegate Road (later called the West Side Territorial Road). The survivors of the Lost Wagon Train soon became established members of existing communities or went on to found neighboring settlements. And what of Elijah Elliott, the so-called guide? Ironically, he became the first road supervisor of Pleasant Hill District No. 10.

A HOMESTEAD CHRISTMAS

The Thomas Kincaid family, including their eldest son Harrison, who would become a prominent Oregon newspaperman, arrived in Eugene City on October 11, 1853. They took a narrow mile-long strip of land for their homestead, all that was left between two other claims, and began building shelter for themselves right away. There was little time for rest after the journey on the Oregon Trail. Working fifteen hours a day, they completed a one-room log cabin and moved in with their five children early in December. Some neighbors gave the children a dog to replace one that had died on the trail.

Leonore Gale Barette, a granddaughter of the Kincaids, preserved invaluable details of the frontier experience in a booklet titled *Christmas in Oregon Territory*. For example, she described how their beds, which attached bench-style to the wall, were covered with the soft tips of fir boughs as a foundation for feather mattresses and quilts. For decoration in their new home, a few plates and pieces of crockery were placed on rough shelves.

There was a little mirror, a tintype of Mrs. Kincaid's parents back in Indiana, the family Bible, and a few books and trinkets.

The days were nearing Christmas and Grandfather and Grandmother . . . were hard put to it to know what to do. They had nothing in the way of food with which to make a dinner festive, only flour, potatoes, a bit of dried fruit and a little brown sugar and some bacon. Their money was practically all spent.

It would have to be a homemade celebration. Near the cabin Harrison built a screen of fir boughs and attached long sticks full of pitch, the commonly used pitchlights. Dried pig-bladders, inflated like balloons, were hidden in the fir screen. Just after dusk on Christmas Eve the children were called to see the sizzling pitchlights. *Pop, pop, pop*, the bladders exploded amid shrieks of laughter. The young ones also received gifts. For Mary Alice there was a small doll, possibly brought from Oregon City. Mr. Kincaid had made a small cane with a carved dog's

head for John.

For supper Mr. Kincaid provided a grouse, and his wife made some little cakes. As a centerpiece "she had contrived a few little figures from potatoes with sticks for legs, and for their faces she scraped the skin from the tuber and had tiny buttons for eyes." After supper the father read from the Bible and explained his understanding of "good will toward men." The evening ended with carols, which he accompanied on his violin.

On that Christmas evening so long ago, the Kincaid family had been in Lane County, in the Territory of Oregon, for only seventy-five days, but they had a snug, warm little cabin, a beautiful hill claim with timber and clear sparkling water; they had some stock and planned to get more; they had a team of good horses, a friendly little dog; the children were in splendid health; a small school had just been started within walking distance over the hills. The road to the future looked promising.

A NEW COUNTY IN A NEW STATE

If I had you in Lane County I'd shoot you! That was a common saying, and it doesn't reflect too well on law and order in the early days of Lane County. Laws may have been more stringently enforced in adjoining jurisdictions, but certainly the populace of Lane County was less rambunctious than that of California and other gold rush areas.

Among the most widespread crimes were drunkenness and selling liquor without a license. Unsupervised animals in the street caused frequent problems. The early courts were also kept busy dealing with horse theft, fistfights, and disputes over land. Lane County, formed in 1851, erected its first jail in 1858, a small stone building near the courthouse in Eugene. Soon, however, local crime became far less pressing an issue than the proposed extension of slavery to the West. A great national upheaval, the War Between the States, lay ahead.

When Oregon became a U.S. Territory

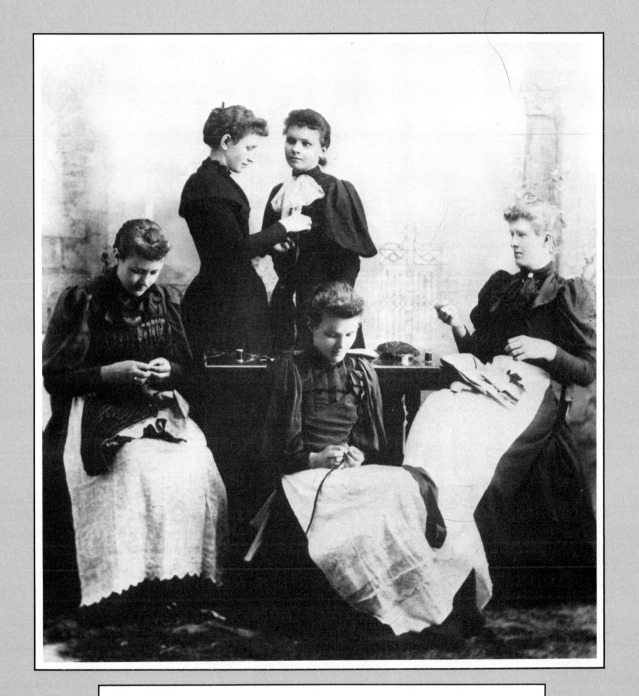

CHAPTER III

*Sewing circles, like this one in 1895, were good oppor-
tunities for women to talk about issues important to
them, and very likely the right of suffrage was among
the topics most discussed. Courtesy, Lane County Historical Museum*

Left: *General Joseph Lane, appointed the first governor of the Oregon Territory in 1848, enjoyed enormous popularity until the issue of slavery, which he favored, reached the West. Courtesy, Dot Dotson's*

Right: *John Whiteaker, an outspoken Lane County farmer, was elected the first governor of the State of Oregon. Courtesy, Dot Dotson's*

in 1848, President James K. Polk appointed General Joseph Lane, an Indiana politician and hero of the Mexican-American War, as territorial governor. The post had first been offered to Abraham Lincoln, who refused it, reputedly at his wife's insistence. General Lane, though a supporter of slavery, became enormously popular as governor, especially since he played an active role in the Indian wars. He was a Democrat, and Democrats far outnumbered Republicans in Oregon, due to the shrewd organizational skills of Salem newspaper owner Asahel Bush. Eventually, the issue of slavery created a serious division in the Oregon Democratic party, causing Bush to skewer the governor in the *Oregon Statesman.* Lane subsequently lost much of his support, as general sentiment opposed slavery.

Oregon's involvement in the national debate began in 1854: Congress passed the Kansas-Nebraska Act, which gave territories the right to decide by popular vote whether to allow slavery or not. Three years later, in *Scott v. Sanford,* the Supreme Court declared it illegal for territorial governments to prohibit slavery;

only a state government was entitled to do so. Most Oregonians had been reluctant to support statehood, fearing heavy taxation. To prevent slavery in Oregon, they quickly voted to call a constitutional convention. In the fall of 1857 a constitution was presented for voter approval, which it received. Citizens voted against slavery and also voted to prohibit the residence of free blacks (a provision rendered invalid after the Civil War).

It wasn't until 1859 that Oregon was admitted to the Union. Congress hesitated for two years because of the slavery issue and because Republicans wished to prevent the addition of a Democratic state to the Union. They needn't have feared. In the 1860 election Abraham Lincoln, a Republican, carried the new state.

Oregon's first elected governor was John Whiteaker, a crusty temperamental farmer from Lane County. Although his personal sympathies leaned toward the South, Oregon officially maintained its allegiance to the Union. Several volunteer regiments were organized in Lane County during the Civil War but were never

JOAQUIN MILLER: AN EARLY LANE COUNTY EXPORT

One of Lane County's most colorful characters, Joaquin Miller became world famous as the self-proclaimed Poet of the Sierras. Courtesy, Lane County Historical Museum

"I am not a liar, I simply exaggerate the truth."

—Joaquin Miller

Oregon pioneer, California gold miner, and internationally known writer, Joaquin Miller was a liar in the best nineteenth-century tradition of tall tales. He made a legend of himself, but he was more than a poseur. Miller wrote thirty-two books, most of them best-sellers; his plays were smash hits on Broadway; and his poetry brought him acclaim as the American Tennyson. For years schoolchildren throughout the United States have memorized his most famous poem, "Columbus," repeating, "Sail on! sail on! sail on! and on!"

Before he changed his name to Joaquin (taken from California desperado Joaquin Murietta), Miller was Cincinnatus Hiner Miller, born in Indiana in 1839. He moved with his family in 1852 to a homestead east of Coburg in Lane County but soon ran away to California, where he cooked for the miners, fought Indians, married an Indian and fathered her child, stole a horse, went to jail, escaped, returned to Oregon, and went to Columbia College in Eugene.

In 1863 he bought the *Democratic Register,* which quickly failed due to hostility toward its Southern sentiments. Meanwhile Joaquin had fallen in love by mail with poet Minnie Myrtle Dyer, "the sweet singer of the Coquille," and married her. No longer welcome in Eugene because of his newspaper, the couple went to Canyon City, a gold boom town in eastern Oregon, where he became a judge and Indian fighter. In his spare time he wrote poetry. His wife gave birth to three children while he had several affairs. They returned to Eugene and separated.

Miller went to San Francisco, where he began to tout himself as a celebrity poet. For publicity he sailed to England and laid a wreath on Byron's tomb. He also used the last of his funds to self-publish a volume of poems, anonymously. When the London critics claimed the poems were written by Robert Browning, Miller stepped forward and became an overnight sensation as the poet of the Sierras. He invented a Wild West costume for himself—long, flowing hair and beard, buckskins, knives and pistols, a dashing hat, and Indian beads—the very costume his friend Buffalo Bill Cody used for his cowboy and Indian show.

Miller was presented to Queen Victoria and rubbed elbows with the leading poets and artists of his day, including the beautiful actress Lily Langtry. Without bothering to divorce Minnie, he married heiress Abbie Leland, moved to Washington, D.C., and had another daughter. When that arrangement didn't work out, Miller moved to Oakland, California, making frequent visits to Oregon. His son Harry robbed a stagecoach and was sentenced to three years in San Quentin. Miller denied the relationship, calling his son an imposter.

During his later years Miller campaigned for the preservation of Crater Lake as a national park and for the rights of Indians. At the age of sixty he traveled to the Yukon as a reporter on the Klondike gold rush.

If some readers claimed Browning had written Miller's poems, his estranged wife Minnie claimed that she was the author of many of them. She toured Oregon giving popular lectures about women's suffrage and about the terrible ways of her famous husband.

Miller's brother George was important in Lane County as a real estate developer, launching the city of Florence and adding many homes to Eugene. Because of Joaquin's strong roots in Lane County, residents have always considered him one of their own.

Harrison Kincaid, founder of the Oregon State Journal, *was a prominent newspaperman for many years in Lane County. Courtesy, Dot Dotson's*

called into active service, partly because of the distance and partly because of the periodic threat of Indian wars. Some men went East and joined regiments there.

A number of Lane County Confederate sympathizers were eager to fight, even on home ground. They formed the "Long Tom Confederacy," drawing members from small settlements by the West Side Territorial Road. When John Mulkey marched into Eugene with a group of "Confederates" looking for a fight, he was summarily taken into custody and sent up to Vancouver Barracks in Washington state. The government sent troops from Vancouver with a small cannon, and the matter quickly died down.

The Civil War was fought in Oregon with editorial rather than artillery blasts by well established newspapers in Portland, Salem, and Oregon City. By the start of the war several papers had come and gone in Eugene, among them the *News,* published by John B. Alexander, and the *Pacific Journal,* which became the *People's Press* under B.J. Pengra. Pugnacious Pengra, later appointed Surveyor General of Oregon by President

Lincoln, was not averse to using his fists if words were insufficient to support the North's cause.

In 1863 the *Democratic Register* was purchased by young Joaquin Miller, who later became world famous as a self-aggrandizing poet. His romance with the Confederacy was so unappreciated in Lane County that civic leaders strongly urged him to leave town, which he did, easily finding employment as a judge in eastern Oregon.

Harrison Kincaid worked on several Eugene newspapers before he founded, in 1864, the *Oregon State Journal,* which would occupy a prominent position in Lane County for nearly four decades. That was a good year to start a newspaper because the telegraph had come to the county and, for the first time, the news was still new when it was printed. In 1867 John Alexander, undaunted by the failure of the *News,* started the *Eugene City Guard,* which became the town's other important newspaper for many years.

The *Eugene Register,* a Republican paper founded in 1883, instigated a lengthy political battle with the Democratic *Guard.* The conflict ended amicably in their merger in 1930 as the *Eugene Register-Guard,* now simply the *Register-Guard.*

Springfield's first newspaper was the short-lived *Springfield Messenger,* published in the 1890s by Frank and Will Gilstrap. The *Nonpareil,* founded in 1896 by John Wood, was the forerunner of the present *Springfield News.*

There was nothing bland, or even impartial, about the early newspapers. The "Oregon Style" of journalism became known around the country. According to historian Dr. Edwin R. Bingham, the Oregon Style was "a species of storm-and-stress composition, strong chiefly in invective." In this era, when nearly everyone knew everyone else in the community, journalists took any opportunity to coin amusing and offensive titles for their opponents. Today such writing would be classified as slanderous, if not obscene, and would undoubtedly cause a rash of lawsuits and countersuits.

Oregon newspapers took such an ambiguous, or even hostile, stand on women's suffrage that the state's outstanding suffragist, Abigail Scott Duniway, started her own newspaper in 1871. Her Portland-based weekly *New Northwest* reached subscribers all over the state. In Lane County both urban and rural women supported Duniway as a frequent and spirited speaker, although she was on more than one occasion locked out of lecture halls by opponents. Susan B. Anthony toured the area, and local poet Minnie Myrtle Miller, estranged wife of Joaquin Miller, also spoke in favor of women's suffrage.

The Lane County newspaper most vociferous in opposition was the *Eugene City Guard,* which called the feminists "she-roosters," "strong-minded females," and "the vinegarfaced squad." Harrison Kincaid was more sympathetic in his *Oregon State Journal,* prompting the *Guard* to editorialize in 1872 that

Kincaid was overly fond of the brilliant Mrs. Duniway.

The Oregon State Women's Suffrage Association was strong enough in Lane County to effect local passage of the women's suffrage measure in 1900, but the issue didn't pass statewide until 1912, after its sixth appearance on the ballot. Abigail Scott Duniway, at the age of seventy-seven, was the first Oregon woman registered to vote. In spite of the length of the battle, women in Oregon achieved suffrage eight years before ratification of the Nineteenth Amendment.

While women struggled for suffrage,

The Junction City Bulletin *was one of several newspapers that sprang up during the 1860s, the era of the "Oregon Style" of no-holds-barred journalism. Courtesy, Lane County Historical Museum*

After forty-two years of leading the fight for women's suffrage, Abigail Scott Duniway registered in 1912 as the first female voter in Oregon. Courtesy, Oregon Historical Society (neg. no. Oregonian 4599)

Indians waged a separate battle for their rights. Although no Indian wars took place in Lane County, numerous residents (perhaps feeling left out of the Civil War) joined volunteer regiments to fight in most of the eight wars against various tribes between 1847 and 1878. The Rogue River War, fought in southwestern Oregon between 1851 and 1856, had the most impact on Lane County because it interfered with travel to the gold fields in that area and in California.

The Kalapuya, Siuslaw, and Molalla tribes of Lane County signed treaties in 1855 that assigned them to reservations.

In the 1880s, some Indian children were placed in training schools such as this one in Chemawa, Oregon. They were educated and trained in white people's ways and occupations. Courtesy, Oregon Historical Society (neg. no. 36112)

The Siuslaws remained on their own land on the coast because it was part of the Siletz Reservation. The inland Willamette Valley Indians were moved near the coast north of Lane County to the tiny Grand Ronde Reservation.

Indian agents Anson Dart and Joel Palmer argued successfully that it would be disastrous to relocate the Indians east of the Cascade Mountains, where they would perish in the arid environment. However, the land finally allotted for the reservations was considered undesirable

by settlers and unsuitable for farming. Here the Indians were expected to learn how to farm and become self-supporting.

Even the reservation land became coveted as more settlers entered Oregon. Part of the Siletz land was removed from the reservation in 1865, and in 1875 an act of Congress threw open a major section for white settlement, which led to the devlopment of Florence and the Lane County coastal area.

Meanwhile, the settlers were anxious to formalize the organization of towns. In 1862 many residents of Eugene City were ready to incorporate, primarily to "banish the common nuisances, hogs and grog-shops, from the town"; the *State Republican* took a skeptical view of the proposal: "as to maintaining a city government merely to get rid of a few old sows that might perambulate the streets, that would be a very expensive way of accomplishing a small amount of good."

Nevertheless the city did incorporate on October 17, 1862. In 1864 a new charter changed the name to City of Eugene and designated two-year terms for municipal officials: president, six trustees, recorder, marshal, and treasurer. The president and trustees were to receive no salary, as the mayor and councilors today receive none. Eugene's first officers were J.B. Underwood, president; J.A. McClung, Eugene F. Skinner, F.B. Dunn, C.C. Croner, William T. Osburn, T.G. Hendricks, trustees; Alonzo A. Skinner, recorder; Bell Jennings, treasurer; and C.H. Fox, marshal. Thomas Chase filled the added office of street commissioner.

Also in 1862 Eugene made its second bid to become Oregon's capital. The first had come in 1856, when various cities competed in an election to relocate the territorial capital. Eugene received a majority, but the legislature decided the vote was nonbinding and the capital remained at Salem. Again in 1862 Eugene received a majority, but apparently Salem officials refused to release the poll

For Indian children in the training school at Forest Grove, Oregon, education began with uniform dress and haircuts. The photograph below shows a group of children who had just arrived at the school. Courtesy, Oregon Historical Society (neg. nos. 2655 and 65709)

books in a timely manner and the vote was declared invalid. Finally in 1864 Salem received a clear majority, and the capital has remained there. Understandably there was considerable bitterness among early Eugeneans toward Salem and the powerful "Salem Clique," led by newspaperman Asahel Bush.

Eugene was somewhat mollified when, after long and concerted effort on the part of local citizens, the Oregon legislature passed an act in 1872 creating a state university to be "permanently located at the town of Eugene City."

The quality of life was enhanced not only by the opening of the university in 1876 but also by enactment of an unusual city ordinance. Somehow it had become a tradition in Eugene to toll the courthouse bell immediately after the death of a citizen, day or night. The city council declared in 1876 that the bells were injurious to the health of people who were ill and to the nerves of women and children and resolved that "the tolling of the bell at the death of a person is a custom unknown anywhere else, except on extraordinary occasions, and we condemn the practice."

The city grew, and matured. It was deemed necessary in 1879 to pay a salary of $75 per month to the city treasurer. Council President B.F. Dorris reported

only fifteen arrests during that year. Apparently Eugene was settling down, as were other Lane County towns. Springfield was incorporated in 1885; Cottage Grove and Florence followed suit in 1893. During the 1880s the Lane County Commissioners devoted much of their time to voting on right-of-ways for roads, railroads, power lines, and the county's picturesque covered bridges. The Military and Territorial roads formed the basis of the county road system.

TWO HANGINGS

Claude Branton was hanged in 1899 for the murder of John Linn. Sheriff Whithers is the tall man on the right. Courtesy, Lane County Historical Museum

A select group of Lane County citizens received invitations to view the hanging of Sheriff Whithers' murderer, Elliott Lyons, in 1903. Courtesy, Lane County Historical Museum

Legal hangings in Lane County were performed outside the courthouse until 1903, when the state legislature enacted a law requiring all executions to take place inside the state penitentiary in Salem.

The first hanging in Lane County occurred on May 12, 1899, when murderer Claude Branton went peacefully to his death. Branton and a friend, Courtney Green, had both been engaged to women in the McKenzie River area. Needing money to get married, they worked out a plan to kill and rob John Linn, a wealthy cattleman. Branton and Green lured their victim to an isolated camp, thinking he would be carrying at least $1,000. After Linn fell asleep, Branton put a bullet through his heart. The two men took Linn's long buckskin wallet and valuables, only to discover that he had a mere $100. They burned the body in a bonfire, while all night Branton played his harmonica. The next day they crushed the bones and buried them in a box. Branton disappeared, but Green turned himself in.

Sheriff William W. Whithers, renowned as a lawman and considered something of a Wyatt Earp and Sherlock Holmes rolled into one, rushed to the scene of the crime, where he found Linn's suspender buttons in the campfire ashes. The sheriff then questioned residents along the McKenzie, who testified that they had seen Branton trying to pose as his victim, wearing whiskers made of a horse's tail. By intercepting a letter from Branton to his girlfriend, Sheriff Whithers learned when the fugitive was returning to the area. As soon as Branton appeared in Eugene, Whithers promptly arrested him.

In jail Branton kept a diary. "Three can keep a secret only when two are dead," he wrote. When he went to the scaffold, he advised the crowd to "follow the right."

The murder of Sheriff Whithers was the reason for Lane County's last hanging. In February 1903, he and his constable went to Walton, twenty-nine miles west of Eugene, to arrest Elliott Ellis Lyons for horse theft. The constable guarded the back door. The sheriff went into the living room, where he found Lyons with his pregnant wife and his parents. A scuffle ensued. Lyons shot Whithers in the throat and made his escape through the snow and mud. The popular sheriff died thirty-six hours later.

Lyons was caught in Creswell on February 9, four days after the shooting. The *Eugene Guard* reported that "if it is the intention to let him await the March term of circuit court his life would not be worth thirty cents in this city." A group of deputies successfully guarded him from a bloodthirsty mob outside the county jail. Lyons was convicted in a one-day trial on March 4, sentenced on March 6, and hanged in the county courtyard on April 17, 1903.

A select group of citizens received formal invitations to witness the hanging from inside a fence built around the gallows. The reason for putting up the enclosure remains unclear. The scaffold stood higher than the fence, and a huge crowd outside had an unobstructed view of Lane County's last hanging.

A new Lane County Courthouse was built in 1898-1899 for less than $50,000. The brick structure served as county seat for over fifty years before it was, unfortunately, torn down. The present four-story courthouse, costing over $2 million, was dedicated in 1959.

Across from the courthouse are the park blocks. When Charnelton Mulligan donated forty acres for the founding of Eugene City, he specified four acres for use as a county courthouse and its surroundings. Traditionally the park blocks have provided a center for public gatherings. The area served as Eugene's first marketplace, fairgrounds, and concert stage. In the early part of this century a comfortable rest cottage was located there for the convenience of farm women who traveled into Eugene for a day of shopping. When the new courthouse was built, redesign of the park blocks elicited many complaints about the removal of the old horseshoe pits. Recently the park has been the scene of Eugene's Saturday Market.

Attached to the courthouse is Harris Meeting Hall, named in honor of Judge Lawrence T. Harris, a native Oregonian who, in addition to two terms as circuit judge, served on the state supreme court from 1914 to 1924. Another outstanding Lane County judge similarly honored was Judge G.F. Skipworth, for whom Skipworth Home, the county juvenile detention center, was renamed in 1950.

The distinguished attorney Edward F. Bailey chaired the committee that wrote the home rule charter for Lane County. Before the Oregon legislature passed the County Home Rule Amendment in 1958, each county government had the same structure and had no legislative power. In 1962 Lane County joined the small percentage of county governments in the United States that have home rule charters.

Dr. Bailey, a native of Junction City, enjoyed lifelong popularity throughout

Oregon. As a 235-pound tackle he was one of the University of Oregon's earliest football heroes. After law school he coached football at Albany College and later served as a state representative and state senator.

The Lane County politician best known on the national level was Senator Wayne L. Morse, the "tiger of the Senate." Morse was dean of the University of Oregon Law School before his election to the Senate as a Republican in 1944. Never a blind partisan, he left the Republican party in 1952, serving as an Independent, and then joined the Democrats in 1955. Revered by many and hated by others, he was a strong advocate of civil rights, organized labor, and federal aid to education. He relentlessly opposed U.S. intervention in Vietnam. Morse died while campaigning in 1974. His home in south Eugene, the Morse Ranch, is now a park.

Henry Cook's vegetable stall, shown here circa 1917, was part of the first marketplace at the park blocks in central Eugene. Today the Saturday Market, a crafts fair, takes place in the same location. Courtesy, Lane County Historical Museum

EUGENE AND SPRINGFIELD: GROWING INTO CITIES

When the small sternwheeler *James Clinton* puffed up the Willamette and docked at Skinner's Butte on March 12, 1856, nearly every man, woman, child, and dog in Eugene turned up for the event. There was good reason to cheer. Eugene and Lane County would have real transportation at last. Never mind that the first trip required three days from Corvallis, forty miles away. Never mind that the merchants of Eugene and Harrisburg in Linn County had to promise a substantial investment in the boat when it arrived. It was worth the $5,000.

Transportation was the key to economic development. At that time the roads were virtually impassable to wagons during eight months of the year, so the river was the best means for moving produce and lumber out and, just as important, for bringing manufactured goods in. Bolts of colorful calico meant that women no longer had to spin, weave, and dye their cloth. A

Building the railroad meant tunneling through mountainous sections of Lane County, as illustrated by the work of a crew from Oakridge in 1912. During the nineteenth century and early twentieth century, transportation was the key to economic development. Courtesy, Lane County Historical Museum

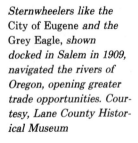

Lane County women had to spin, weave, and dye their own cloth before river boats began bringing supplies of manufactured goods up the Willamette River. Courtesy, Lane County Historical Museum

host of other common products brought equally revolutionary improvements in frontier living.

When Eugene Skinner selected his land claim in 1846, he assumed the Willamette River would provide easy transportation, as in the East and Midwest. However, the river proved surprisingly shallow. After 1856 two companies, the People's Transportation Company and the Willamette Steamboat Company, plied its waters to Eugene, but during the dry summer months most boats were unable to navigate so far upriver.

Even farther upriver, Springfield had been built with the same belief that river transportation would bring prosperity, but only rarely did a steamer reach its

docks—and that was during heavy flooding. On December 29, 1861, the water was high enough for the steamer *Relief* to take on thirteen tons of freight.

In 1874 Captain U.B. Scott constructed a shallow-draft steamer to operate on the Willamette. Drawing only eight inches, the *Ohio* proved successful, even though its stern wheel occasionally fell off and drifted downriver. A boat would be lowered to go after it, the men would set it back in place, and the steamer would continue on its way.

Steamboating was slow and unpredictable. For passengers the alternative was the stagecoach. When Lane County service began in 1857, Renfrew Tavern on the corner of Willamette and Broadway served as the main stop in Eugene. The stages ran north and south until the railroad to California was completed in 1887; the Eugene to Mapleton route continued until 1916.

By stagecoach it could take four days to drive from Ashland to Portland, approximately 300 miles. Consequently, travel was done out of necessity, not for pleasure, and passengers often chose to walk over certain notorious sections, especially the corduroy roads made of tree trunks laid side by side.

The trip to Mapleton, which takes less than an hour by car today, lasted four-

Sternwheelers like the City of Eugene and the Grey Eagle, shown docked in Salem in 1909, navigated the rivers of Oregon, opening greater trade opportunities. Courtesy, Lane County Historical Museum

teen hours under the best conditions. The stagecoach departed from Eugene and traveled twenty-three miles west; passengers then switched to low, open buckboard wagons, which didn't tip over as easily on the primitive mountain road. Three miles outside of Mapleton most passengers got off and walked along a path into town, while the wagon wound along thirteen miles of twisting road before reaching its destination. From Mapleton, continuing passengers could take a boat to Florence.

Narrow, winding roads made overland travel and shipping a rough, often perilous proposition. Courtesy, Lane County Historical Museum

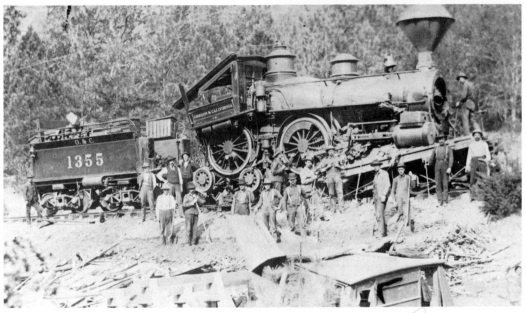

The railroad, although not without its hazards, was a vast improvement over steamboats and stagecoaches, providing regular schedules of freight and passenger service. Courtesy, Lane County Historical Museum

Even more important than a coastal connection in the early days was a route to the East, especially to the gold fields of Idaho. In 1862 Eugene businessmen hired Felix Scott, Jr., and John Cogswell to rough out a Cascades road through the lava beds of McKenzie Pass. It took twenty-six oxen to pull a wagon over this route, but somehow the road builders managed to drive 900 cattle across.

Willamette Pass provided a more practical route east for the Oregon Central Military Wagon Road, begun in 1864 and completed in 1867. A congressional land grant of six sections for every mile of road built subsidized the project, with B.J. Pengra, the Surveyor General and

former newspaper publisher, in charge of construction. Cattle and sheep raisers drove their livestock along this road to the Boise market for many years.

After the railroads came to Lane County both the steamboats and the stagecoaches were doomed to become romantic

By 1912, five trains a day traveled between the Eugene depot and Portland, transforming the economy and making travel a pleasant experience. Courtesy, Lane County Historical Museum

A Locomobile purchased by E.H. Ingham, owner of the Ax Billy department store, created quite a stir in Lane County in 1903. Courtesy, Lane County Historical Museum

William Smith, riding in style in 1912, is reputed to have owned the first Cadillac in Lane County. Courtesy, Lane County Historical Museum

relics. Ambitious business owners, foreseeing that the railroad would transform the economy of the region, were glad to encourage a modern means of transportation. The coming of the iron horse held as much excitement and hope as the space program does today.

In October 1871, the Oregon and California Railroad, building south from Portland, reached Lane County, and farmers and loggers began to enjoy real economic growth. Although the O & C Railroad went bankrupt in 1885, it was

taken over by Southern Pacific, which completed connections to California in 1887. Springfield was added to the rail network in 1891.

Travel was no longer a miserable chore —it was now a pleasant excursion, and people were going places. By 1912 the Oregon Electric Railway and Southern Pacific provided five daily trains between Eugene and Portland. The Electric was the longest interurban electric railway in Oregon and one of the few in the country to offer sleeping-car service.

With the development of the automobile, road building again gained importance. Even the railroads encouraged good roads as a means of trucking produce and livestock short distances to railroad terminals, where the goods were loaded onto trains for long hauls. No one imagined that eventually an interstate network of highways would offer direct competition with the railroads.

The first horseless carriages were looked upon as extravagant toys for adults, as a novelty. In 1903 E.H. Ingham, owner of the Ax Billy department store, bought a steam-powered Locomobile. The

LANE COUNTY'S COVERED BRIDGES

Covered bridges can be seen throughout western Oregon, but Lane County in particular is known for its graceful and homey wooden structures. The twenty-one extant covered bridges were built and are maintained by Lane County. Although there are subtle differences of design and construction among them, all feature the Howe truss, vertical-batten siding, roof-line windows, and painted white exteriors.

Most of the bridges were built in the 1920s and 1930s, many replacing earlier structures. Some are no longer open to motorized traffic because today's loads are heavier than in the days of the Model T. Local groups have been successful in preserving most of Lane County's covered bridges.

The earliest record of covered-bridge construction in Oregon dates back to 1851, when one was built at Oregon City. Bridges were covered with house-like structures because in a rainy climate the trusses and the plank decking lasted longer under cover and even strengthened with age.

One of Oregon's most frequently photographed covered bridges is the Goodpasture Bridge on the McKenzie River, thirty-four miles east of Springfield. Built in 1939, it is 165 feet long. Other covered bridges along the McKenzie are Horse Creek Bridge, built in 1930, and Belknap Bridge, built in 1966. Belknap, the most recently constructed covered bridge in Oregon, replaced a 1939 bridge washed out in the 1964 flood.

In the Fall Creek area are Pengra Bridge and Unity Bridge. Pengra Bridge, built in 1938, contains two of the longest timbers ever cut for a bridge in Oregon. The lower chords, cut by the Booth-Kelly Lumber Company, measure 16 inches by 18 inches by 126 feet. The town of Lowell has its bridge, and Parvin Bridge is located close to Dexter.

Near Cottage Grove three bridges cross Mosby Creek, and two others span the Row River. In the Mohawk Valley are Wendling Bridge and Ernest Bridge, which was used in a scene of the Civil War movie *Shenandoah* in the mid-1960s.

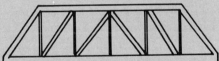

Construction of covered bridges increased after the turn of the century to meet the growing transportation needs of Lane County. Shown is the Hendricks Bridge, circa 1900. Courtesy, Lane County Historical Museum

The Howe truss is a characteristic design element of Lane County covered bridges.

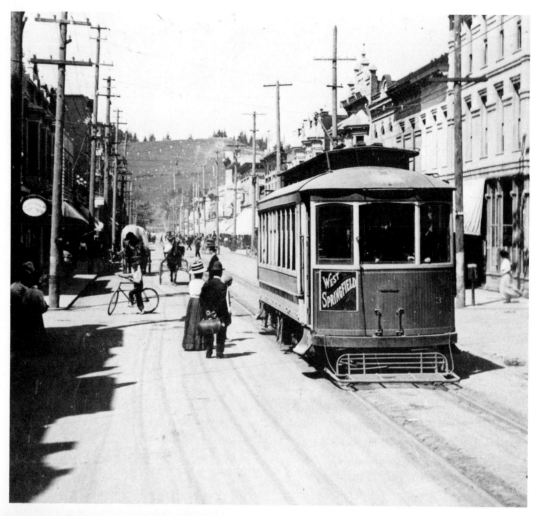

Bicycling was part of the transportation boom in the early years of the century. Shown here is C.C. Matlock's shop in Eugene, circa 1904. Courtesy, Lane County Historical Museum

next year F.S. Chambers had an Autocar shipped out from Chicago, and on the Fourth of July he gave free rides to more than 700 thrill seekers. In 1906, when Eugene had four autos, three university students were booked for exceeding the speed limit of ten miles per hour.

So many places to go; some far away,

some very close. Springfield, the tiny mill town right across the river from Eugene, was quite an attraction between 1910 and 1913. Hundreds of Eugeneans regularly paid six cents to take the electric streetcar over the bridge, past hop yards and a baseball diamond, to reach the bars on Main Street. During those years Eugene had a prohibition ordinance while Springfield remained "wet." By 1912 Springfield had more bars than churches. A sheriff often rode the streetcar back to Eugene to make sure inebriated passengers didn't disturb any women passengers.

Eugene and Springfield, as well as the rest of Lane County, had very sober interests when it came to higher education. The Cumberland Presbyterian Church built Columbia College on College Hill in Eugene in 1856, when the town was still more theory than fact. E.P. Henderson of Pennsylvania served as the college's first president. The original building burned after only four days of classes; the fifty-two students attended classes in a private home until a new building was erected.

That second structure lasted nearly a year, with 100 male students in attendance, before it too burned. Arson was suspected as church members were embroiled in the issue of slavery. Professor Henderson resigned in disgust. He was succeeded as president by Professor Ryan, a southerner who wrote pro-slavery articles for the newspapers. When B.J. Pengra published Harrison Kincaid's rebuttals in the *People's Press,* an enraged Ryan fired a shot at Pengra and then fled the Territory. Columbia College was laid to rest.

Lane County went without a college for the next twenty years. In 1872 leading citizens organized the Union University Association, whose board of directors presented a bill to the state legislature asking permission to establish permanently a state university in Eugene. The bill passed in spite of great opposition from citizens of Albany, who wanted the university for their town. The Eugene directors set out to raise $50,000 for the first university building.

Judge J.J. Walton, T.G. Hendricks, B.F. Dorris, and other organizers went door-to-door soliciting subscriptions. Cash was limited, so people pledged labor, produce, and livestock. Church groups threw fund-raising suppers and strawberry festivals, and schoolchildren saved their pennies. Funds ran out before a roof for the new building was completed. Again the directors had to ask their friends and neighbors for more money. After numerous crises the university opened in 1876. Tuition-free at first, courses of study were offered by a college of literature and arts and a normal college. Three professors and two normal-school teachers handled the entire class load.

Northwest Christian College, located right next to the University of Oregon,

opened in 1895 as the Eugene Divinity School. Its students have always had the advantage of taking classes at both the university and the college through a reciprocal agreement. In 1925 the Bible Standard Theological School, now Eugene Bible College, opened with the Reverend Fred Hornshuh, Sr., as president. South of Eugene and Springfield, Lane Community College was built during 1968-1969 in a beautiful meadow surrounded by wooded hills.

Although Lane County's early settlers organized church congregations within the first few years of their arrival, there was little money for constructing church buildings and paying full-time ministers. Eugene's First Baptist Church, founded in 1852, built its first meeting house in 1867. The Cumberland Presbyterian Church, organized in 1853, built Columbia College before completing its church in 1857.

The four-year existence of Columbia College in Eugene was filled with mishap and disagreement. During the first week of classes the building was destroyed by fire. Courtesy, Dot Dotson's

Other early churches included Saint Mary's Episcopal Church, the First Methodist Church, Eugene Presbyterian Church, and the First Christian Church. The 1880s and 1890s brought a flurry of construction as many new congregations formed. Most of Eugene's older churches

First Baptist Church members originally conducted services in the home of the Mahlon Harlow family. The first meeting hall, built in 1867, was followed in 1927 by this second building, which is still in use. Courtesy, Dot Dotson's

have been replaced by contemporary structures, but a notable exception is the First Christian Church at 1166 Oak Street. This large Classic Revival building was constructed in 1911.

Springfield's first church, the Baptist Church, was built in 1871 on the corner of Second and C streets. Ebbert Memorial (United Methodist) Church, listed in the State Historic Inventory, was built in 1916 at 532 C Street. It retains much of its original interior and features stained-glass windows by the Povey Brothers of Portland.

The settlers formed secular as well as religious associations. Eugene City was barely established when the Masons

Above: The Eugene Divinity School, forerunner of the Northwest Christian College, was located at Twelfth and Kincaid in Eugene, near the University of Oregon campus. Courtesy, Lane County Historical Museum

Right: The Commercial Club, forerunner of the Chamber of Commerce, promoted the business climate of the Lane County area. Courtesy, Dot Dotson's

organized a chapter in 1856 with a membership of ninety-eight. The Masonic Cemetery at the end of University Street was the first in town. Eugene's Independent Order of Odd Fellows (IOOF) lodge began meeting in 1860; Springfield built its lodge in 1881. Dozens of clubs and organizations, some local and some with national affiliation, sprang up to deal with problems of crime, poverty, health, and civic improvement or to promote causes such as temperance, women's suffrage, and high culture. The Chamber of Commerce originated as the Commercial Club in 1902. For years it published a

booster pamphlet called *Anybody's Magazine,* which extolled the business climate of Lane County.

The notorious Ku Klux Klan made an appearance in Oregon's urban areas in the early 1920s. Since there were few target minorities in the state at that time, Klan activity was mainly confined to lobbying against private schools, most of which were Catholic. In Lane County the movement died down after a few years, although racism again came to the fore during World War II, when Japanese and Japanese-American residents, mostly from the Portland and Hood River areas, were evacuated to a temporary relocation center at Portland's Pacific International

Livestock Exposition Building. Some were allowed to move to eastern Oregon, but others were sent to the camp in Tule Lake, California.

When Eugene was still known as Skinner's Mudhole, its public services were few. By the early part of this century Eugene and Springfield had all the services urban dwellers expected. Both had fire departments in the 1880s, and Eugene installed electric streetlights in 1888. A streetcar system began in 1891, and street paving initiated in 1907.

A group of businessmen started a telephone company in 1888 but, with only six subscribers, abandoned the project within a year. After Pacific Telephone and Telegraph ran lines from Portland in 1894, customers enjoyed local service for fifty cents a month.

A typhoid epidemic traced to Eugene's water supply system, which was privately owned, prompted a movement for public utilities. Between 1910 and 1920 numerous service companies and agencies were established, including the Eugene Heating and Electric Power Plant, the Oregon Electric Railway, and the Eugene Water and Electric Board (EWEB). The Eugene Airport, inaugurated in 1919, was the first municipal airport on the Pacific

The volunteer firefighters of Hose Company No. 3 took part in the Fourth of July festivities of 1896, drawing a float in the parade. Courtesy, Dot Dotson's

The crew for the first around-the-world flight landed briefly in Eugene in 1923. Courtesy, Lane County Historical Museum

Coast. The crew of the first around-the-world flight landed there in 1923.

Following Eugene's water scandal, Springfield had its publicly owned water system installed by Willamette Valley Company in 1906. A bond issue to build sewers passed the next year. The cost of water was set at fifty cents a month for each faucet, bathtub, and toilet. Willamette Valley Company also supplied electricity to the city at that time. The McKenzie Telephone Company provided service in Springfield beginning in 1905. Main Street was paved in 1911, and citizens celebrated the event with a masquerade ball on the new thoroughfare. Its theme was "Springfield Paves the Way."

The bridges between Eugene and Springfield and in adjacent areas had to be rebuilt several times due to flooding, which was particularly heavy in the years 1861 and 1862, 1881 and 1882, 1890, and 1927. The residents of Glenwood, a low area between Eugene and Springfield, were deluged with almost predictable regularity and occasionally took up temporary residence at McArthur Court, the

sports auditorium at the University of Oregon. The Portland District of the Corps of Engineers reported that severe flooding could be expected every five years.

When Congress passed the Flood Control Act in 1936, local authorities were eager to start dam construction. Beginning in 1940 the Corps of Engineers built nine storage reservoirs in Lane County—Fern Ridge, Cottage Grove, Dorena, Lookout Point, Dexter, Fall Creek, Hills Creek, Cougar, and Blue River. Although no heavily populated areas required evacuation because of the construction, a number of early homesteads had to be abandoned. At the time, the loss of the homesteads was considered a small price to pay for security against floods, which caused damage to thousands of farms. The reservoirs provide not only flood protection but also water for farmers and ranchers during the dry months, hydroelectric power, and scenic recreational areas for boating, hunting, and fishing.

Although Lane County now has the largest hospital between Portland and

Eugene Hospital was founded after the influenza epidemic of 1918 heightened public awareness of the need for medical facilities. Courtesy, Lane County Historical Museum

San Francisco, as well as numerous other medical facilities, health services developed slowly until the burgeoning of population after World War II. Early settlers considered Oregon's climate exceptionally healthful, although there were periodic smallpox epidemics. In 1881 the Eugene City Council authorized construction of a pesthouse, or isolation ward, five miles out of town for patients with highly contagious diseases.

The influenza epidemic of October 1918 took its toll in Lane County, as in the rest of the country, emphasizing the need for better medical care. The Eugene Hospital and Clinic, now called the Eugene Clinic, incorporated in 1922 and opened a modest two-story structure. Today the clinic stresses preventive health care but also maintains a fifty-seven-bed hospital.

The much larger Pacific Christian Hospital was founded in 1924 but by 1933 went bankrupt. In 1936 the Sisters of Saint Joseph of Peace purchased the facility for $50,000 and renamed it Sacred Heart General Hospital. The sisters

proved to be excellent administrators, modernizing and remodeling Sacred Heart several times. In 1982 the structure was extensively expanded, providing 421 beds and the services of over 400 physicians. Patients throughout the southern half of Oregon come to Sacred Heart for care of serious medical problems.

Springfield's McKenzie-Willamette Hospital, expanded in 1983 with a $14.5 million ancillary building, was erected in 1954-1955 as a result of assiduous grass-roots fund-raising by 160 volunteers. The city's first hospital, the Springfield Private Hospital, was estab-

Before effective flood control measures were taken by the Army Corps of Engineers, Glenwood was flooded with almost predictable regularity. Shown is the high water of 1927. Courtesy, Lane County Historical Museum

The Shelton-McMurphey house, one of Lane County's most notable historic homes, stands prominently on Skinner's Butte in this snapshot, circa 1890. In the background is the University of Oregon observatory. Courtesy, Lane County Historical Museum

lished on Main Street in the early part of the century by Mrs. Peter Benson. By 1914 it had given way to the larger Springfield General Hospital, which served the community until 1936, when it was converted into apartments. Located at 846 F Street, the building is now listed in the National Register of Historic Structures.

Although most of Eugene's historic downtown buildings were demolished in the 1950s, many lovely old homes are well preserved. In the Skinner's Butte area are the Shelton-McMurphey house, an elaborately detailed Queen Anne structure (built in 1880), the Rural Gothic Cogswell-Miller house (1884), the Pliny Snodgrass house (1880s), and the J.O. Watts house (1893).

Another Queen Anne structure loved by local residents is the Calkins house, built on Eleventh Avenue in 1902 for W.W. Calkins, a prominent banker. Also on Eleventh is the Dr. A.W. Patterson house, built in 1903 and used in 1979 as the set-

ting for the film *Animal House.*

The Fairmount area near Hendricks Park, developed in the 1890s by George Melvin Miller (brother of Joaquin Miller), has many fine hillside houses, a good number of them built in the 1920s and 1930s; in recent years others have been constructed high on the slopes in contemporary styles. A home designed by Frank Lloyd Wright, one of the few Wright buildings in Oregon, is located in south Eugene.

In west Eugene the Frank Chambers house from 1892 stands out for its ornamental woodwork. Chambers, a hardware merchant, helped establish the Eugene Woolen Mill, Eugene Opera House, and the YMCA. In southwest Eugene on Lincoln Street is the Peters-Liston-Wintermeier house, begun in 1869 and now considered one of Oregon's finest examples of the Rural Gothic style. Also on Lincoln is the Lansdowne house from the 1890s, featuring well preserved, richly carved woodwork.

On the University of Oregon campus the two original buildings, Deady Hall (built 1873-1876) and Villard Hall (1886), are both on the National Register of Historic Structures. Downtown Eugene enjoys the renovated charms of the Smeede Hotel (1884-1885); the Quackenbush Building (1902); the Lane Building (1903); the Southern Pacific Railroad Depot (1908); the Oregon Electric Depot (1914), now a restaurant; and the Fifth Street district, developed in the early 1900s and renovated in the 1970s.

In downtown Springfield are the IOOF Building (1907); the recently refurbished Pacific Power and Light Building (1908), now the Springfield Museum; the Bell Theater (1910); the Stevens-Perkins Building (1911); and the Springfield Armory (1921). The Southern Pacific Depot (1891), a wood-frame Queen Anne structure with a small second story, is the oldest depot of its type in Oregon.

Outstanding Springfield houses include the Rural Gothic Campbell house (1873), the Brattain-Hadley house (1893), the Stewart house (1906), the elegant Douglas house (1908), and the Innis house (1910). The William Stevens house (1851) is possibly the oldest in Lane County.

Downtown areas throughout the country have been made over in recent years in response to the success of suburban shopping centers. Locally, construction of the enclosed Valley River Center in north Eugene prompted the city's 1971 remodeling of its downtown into a pleasant pedestrian mall, with landscaped walkways, attractive play equipment, and a massive concrete fountain-sculpture at its center. The fountain has been used effectively as a centerpiece for theatrical and musical performance. Holiday celebrations on the mall have also been well attended. Nevertheless, concern about vacancies has brought forth proposals for enclosing the

The Springfield Private Hospital, the city's first medical facility, was founded by Mrs. Peter Benson. Courtesy, Lane County Historical Museum

The Peters-Liston-Wintermeier house, shown here circa 1900, is an outstanding example of the Rural Gothic architectural style. Particularly noteworthy is the vertical board and batten detail. Courtesy, Lane County Historical Museum

Springfield's Southern Pacific Railroad Depot, built in 1891, remains one of the oldest of its type in Oregon. These men await their train circa 1910. Courtesy, Lane County Historical Museum

mall, developing adjacent property into an enclosed mall, or even reverting to the original streets.

During the 1970s Eugene's civic center was additionally transformed by the construction of numerous structures, among them the Atrium Building, Citizens Building, South Park Building, Federal Office Building and Courthouse, and Public Service Building. In 1982 the $20-million Eugene Centre opened for business, comprising the Hult Center for the Performing Arts, the Eugene Hilton Hotel, and the Conference Center.

Springfield's small downtown area has declined over the years for retail business. Shoppers generally prefer Valley River Center or the Springfield Mall, a smaller shopping center in the northern part of the city. However, city commission members are pursuing several plans for revitalization. In 1984 the Downtown Commission recommended the creation of historic districts, including commercial and adjacent residential areas. The commission also recommended more landscaping, a change in traffic patterns, and increased emphasis on attracting offices and service businesses.

To enhance the character of proposed improvements downtown, Springfield has many buildings from the early part of this century that could be restored to their original style, as was the Pacific Power and Light Building when it was converted into the Springfield Museum in 1981. The museum renovation was part of an unusual conversion project. Instead of building a new city hall and library from the ground up, the city purchased an elevated shopping center where business was waning and completely remodeled it into an attractive administrative complex. Springfield is a member of the National Main Street program, which provides a variety of services for protecting and improving downtown areas.

Concern with the quality of life is a major theme in Lane County. There is an increasing awareness that the remaining historic buildings are treasures. Development and growth are guided by the Metro Plan, an evolving set of community goals for containing city services within urban boundaries and for preserving neighborhoods. Preservation of old trees in addition to new planting, construction of an Emerald Canal through Eugene, and creation of a greenway along Springfield's millrace are among the topics being considered by local citizens for the future.

The beautifully preserved Oregon Electric Station is open to the public today as a restaurant. Courtesy, Lane County Historical Museum

THE CHANGING ECONOMY: FROM TIMBER TO TOURISM

Buster Keaton came to Lane County in the 1920s to make *The General,* a spectacular silent film. John Belushi learned to sing the blues while filming *Animal House* in Eugene. Susan Saint James bought a Lane County hideaway after completing *How to Beat the High Cost of Living,* and sportswriter Kenny Moore returned to his alma mater, the University of Oregon, to film *Personal Best.*

Moviemaking is a small but growing part of Lane County's economy. The film companies are attracted to the scenery, and that same scenery, a wealth of timber-covered slopes, makes Lane County the lumber capital of the United States.

The first settlers gave only passing thought to the rich forests that surrounded the fertile valleys where they built their homesteads. Their main concern was agriculture: the Willamette Valley was ideally suited for growing wheat, fruit, and vegetables. After the bottomlands were taken up, settlers began claiming the

Before the advent of the railroad, loggers known as river rats herded logs downstream for milling. With modernized transportation, lumber overtook farming as Lane County's largest industry. Courtesy, Lane County Historical Museum

Center: *A massive logjam could be released by finding and dislodging one key log somewhere in the pile. Courtesy, Lane County Historical Museum*

Far right: *Splash dams were constructed on some streams. When the sluice gates were opened, water rushed through, raising the river below sufficiently to move the timber downstream. Courtesy, Lane County Historical Museum*

This train crash was staged for the filming of The General, *a Buster Keaton movie of the 1920s. Courtesy, Lane County Historical Museum*

wooded foothills. These lands were less profitable for farming, but their value became evident when the California Gold Rush created a timber rush. Because there was no adequate means of transportation for either logs or lumber, development of this resource proceeded slowly at first.

Felix Scott built the first known sawmill in the county on the McKenzie River in 1851-1852, but the most important pioneer sawmill was erected in 1852-1853 by Elias Briggs in Springfield. Briggs and his partners invested $10,000 in digging a millrace and constructing well equipped saw and flour mills. Production increased substantially over the years, and the partners sold the mills for a handsome profit in 1865. The new owners named their business the Springfield Manufacturing Company.

By 1870 there were at least eighteen sawmills, gristmills, and woolen mills in Lane County, but most of their products were sold locally. When the railroad arrived from Portland in 1871, local lumber suppliers looked outward to a vastly enlarged market, and wealthy out-of-state lumber companies began to view Lane County as a new source of timber. Transportation had such an effective influence on the development of the lumber industry in Lane County that production

jumped from 744,000 board feet in 1865 to over 3,800,000 in 1875.

Before the railroad, river driving was the common means of transporting logs to a sawmill. A crew of loggers known as river rats herded the logs downriver on runs that could last between one and three months, depending on distance, size of the harvest, and height of the river. Some streams required the construction of splash dams to provide enough force for driving the logs onward. When enough water built up behind the dam, a gate was released, and logs and water came splashing downstream. When log jams occurred, the river rats had to find and dislodge the key log that was choking the flow.

Logs were brought to the river by means of chutes (a dry trough used as a slide down a hill), flumes (water-filled troughs), and skidroads, over which logs were dragged by mules, oxen, or horses. In the 1880s portable steam engines known as steam donkeys began to replace animal power.

Living conditions in early logging

camps were only for the roughest hardiest men, who lived far from town in crowded bunkhouses that no woman was allowed to enter. Nor would she have wanted to. The stench, grime, and lice were sufficient deterrents. Loggers worked ten to twelve hours a day, six days a week, earning about a dollar a day plus room and board.

By the early years of this century, hygiene had advanced a degree: bunkhouses were replaced by dormitories with two men to a room, and there were oilcloths on the tables in the mess hall. Flora Hills, who cooked for her husband's river crew in 1905, noted in her diary: "Had a big venison feed. Fried venison, boiled potatoes, and gravy. Loggers will eat anything if it has enough gravy on it."

As conditions continued to improve, married men lived with their families in small cabins, and many camps had a school, a store, and even church services. When it was time to move the camp to another site, cabins and buildings were sometimes placed on railroad flatcars and moved down the tracks.

One of Lane County's earliest major timbermen was James Isaac Jones. Having saved $600 from working as a butcher, he bought into a sawmill at Saginaw, on the Coast Fork of the Willamette. Within a few years he boosted production from 6,000 to 65,000 board feet a day. To bring logs down from the hills, Jones built a flume that was more than five miles long and descended 1,660 feet. Logs rushed down the flume to the main saw-

A flume, or water-filled trough, was used to transport logs to the mill. Courtesy, Lane County Historical Museum

mill at speeds up to fifty miles an hour. When Jones sold out to the Booth-Kelly Lumber Company in 1898, the price was an astounding $500,000. Jones was thirty-two years old.

In 1877, after the opening of the Siletz Reservation, the Siuslaw River port became a regular stop for schooner traffic, and commercial lumbering found another major outlet. M.E. Saubert and Company constructed a large mill at Acme. In Florence the Meyer and Kyle Company built a much larger operation, which in 1902 produced over 7 million board feet.

The giant of the local lumber companies was Booth-Kelly. Robert A. Booth and the brothers George and Tom Kelly, all native Oregonians, started by purchasing several small mills in southern Oregon. In 1895 they moved their headquarters to Lane County. After buying Jones' mill at Saginaw in 1899, they built a sawmill and small town called Wendling on the Mohawk River. Their Springfield mill, erected in 1902, could cut 250,000 board feet a day and employed a total of 1,000 workers. In 1903 Booth-

Kelly had its most productive year, turning out well over 143 million board feet. The large mill did wonders for Springfield's development. Its population of 353 in 1900 multiplied to nearly 2,000 by 1910. When the Springfield mill burned to the ground on July 28, 1911, over half the population of the town worked for Booth-Kelly. Fortunately the firm began rebuilding the mill a year later.

From the time of the trappers, eastern lumber interests had been aware of the enormous potential for profit offered by the Northwest. The height and girth of the trees, the density of the forests, and the vast acreage available—hundreds of square miles blanketed by virgin forests—enticed the notorious timber barons.

Many timber companies acquired huge tracts of forest land unscrupulously. One favored method was to have employees file homestead claims on timberlands and then pass title to the employer; another was duping veterans out of their Civil War Veterans' scrip, which was worth 160 acres. An enormous acquisition, involving tens of thousands of acres, hinged on the sale of the Oregon and California Railroad, which had received up to twenty square miles of mountain land for each mile of track laid. As federal land grants, these holdings were to have been sold to settlers in 160-acre parcels. But Southern Pacific took over the O & C in 1887 and, ignoring the law, sold the land to Booth-Kelly.

To control these practices, the federal government created forest preserves. A vigorous conservationist, President Theodore Roosevelt later added 148 million acres to the national forests and did much to reform their administration. Today the U.S. Forest Service and the Bureau of Land Management both hold jurisdiction over federally owned forest lands in Lane County.

The Weyerhaeuser Company, the greatest influence in developing and diversifying the lumber industry in the Northwest, had its beginnings in 1858 when Frederick Weyerhaeuser, a young immigrant, bought a bankrupt Illinois

The Springfield mill of the Booth-Kelly lumber company, shown here circa 1940, was a major factor in the city's growth in the early 1900s. Booth-Kelly continued operations until 1959, when the company was sold to Georgia-Pacific. Courtesy, Lane County Historical Museum

Frederick Weyerhaeuser founded a company in 1858 that became a lumber empire over the next fifty years. The Weyerhaeuser Company is now the owner of the largest private inventory of lumber in the world. Courtesy, Weyerhaeuser Company Archives

lumber company. In 1900 Weyerhaeuser established a new company with headquarters in Tacoma and began to buy land and build mills throughout the Northwest. Today the Weyerhaeuser Company owns the world's largest private inventory of timber.

In the late 1920s, the Weyerhaeuser Company began practicing selective logging, for sustained yield, rather than clear cutting, which was the common method. Selective logging took the old growth but left the younger trees standing for future harvest and for control of erosion. Modern logging practice includes extensive replanting of forests with seedlings from superior trees.

Because of the productivity of Weyerhaeuser and other companies, and because of standing merchantable timber estimated at 95 billion board feet, Lane County is considered the lumber capital of the United States. Weyerhaeuser led the way, building its Springfield mill in 1949 and providing much-needed jobs during the post-war population boom. In 1959 Georgia-Pacific bought out Booth-Kelly and expanded operations. Other large companies include Bohemia, Roseboro, and Pope and Talbot. In addition to lumber, wood products such as particleboard, hardboard, and plywood, which are made from materials that used to be discarded as waste, have become an important part of the industry. Forest products account for 80 percent of the county's exports, with an increasing amount going to Pacific Rim countries, especially China.

The first farmers who came to the Willamette Valley declared that it must have been created specially for growing wheat. They were correct in their assessment, though the valley proved just as hospitable to many other crops. A long growing season, an average rainfall of forty-three inches annually, and relatively mild winters combined bountifully with rich bottomland soil. Writing about Lane County

in 1884, historian A.G. Walling gave this description:

Here vast quantities of wheat, oats, barley and hay are annually harvested, while thousands of bushels of luscious apples, pears, plums and cherries are gathered from the luxuriant orchards that abound throughout the region.

The California Gold Rush inflated the market for the valley's wheat, which went south by pack trains. Local flour mills were kept busy, one of the largest being the Springfield Flour Mill, built in 1854 by Elias Briggs. The mill was sold and expanded several times, and by the turn of the century its Snowball brand was highly acclaimed. In 1908 the mill advertised its flour as:

Pure, wholesome, clean, nutritious and excellent, genuine, faultless, worthy, helpful and reliable. Without doubt Snowball Flour makes better buns, biscuits, bread, rolls, pastry, and cake than any other flour on earth.

In the 1880s two specialized crops gained importance: flax and hops. Flax provided seeds for linseed oil and fibers for cloth manufacturing. Hops went into the beer made in German breweries in Portland and Vancouver, Washington. When Prohibition curbed the market for hops in the U.S., farmers sold to European breweries whose hop yards had been destroyed in World War I. The unstable economy of the 1930s, coupled with a devastating mildew epidemic, eventually forced most local hop farmers to plow under their fields and try some other crop.

Filberts, also known as hazelnuts, are a major product first grown in Lane County by George A. Dorris, who was also known around the turn of the century for the quality of his asparagus. In 1908 Oliver Hovey Todd introduced mint, which was so popular as an ingredient in chewing gum that by 1915 farmers sold it at $14 a pound. Apples, cherries, strawberries, prunes, and many other fruits and vegetables have done well as cash crops since the nineteenth century. A more recent arrival, grass seed has stirred some controversy: growers burn their fields each summer, causing complaints from area residents and resulting in stringent regulations.

Chase Gardens, a horticulture firm in Eugene with hundreds of employees, was founded in 1889. Frank B. Chase started out by raising cattle, fruit, and vegetables. In the summer he traveled door-to-door, selling produce from his wagon. Although crops flourished in Lane County without benefit of irrigation, Chase gave it a try during the dry summer months around 1890 and discovered that it brought spectacular results. A half-acre of celery produced more income than two acres of wheat. Chase built wooden flumes for carrying water throughout his acreage, though it was many years before irrigation became widespread.

In 1905 Chase built his first green-house, which increased production considerably; he began growing flowers in 1922. Today millions of carnations, gardenias, and other blooms are shipped around the country. Chase Gardens is renowned for its numerous types of orchids.

Another firm, Greer Gardens, has produced many new strains of rhododendrons, which grow so profusely in Lane County that they could almost be considered the official flower.

The earliest settlers, finding Willamette Valley to be rich in pastureland, began raising sheep and cattle as soon as they arrived in the 1840s. Today that land is generally more valuable for growing crops, although there are still sheep raisers in the valley. Most cattle ranchers have moved their herds to the large ranges in eastern Oregon. Lane County dairy products are sold through Echo Spring Dairy and Dairy Gold Farms. Willamette Poultry in Creswell is a major supplier of fresh chicken in Oregon.

Although commercial fishing and pack-

The Willamette Valley must have been created specially for growing wheat, or so it seemed to the area's first farmers. Courtesy, Lane County Historical Museum

HOP PICKING: LANE COUNTY'S FIRST PAID VACATION

Picking hops was a popular seasonal occupation in the early part of the century. Pickers earned one cent per pound, with 100 to 200 pounds being a daily average. Oregon became the world's leading hop producer in the 1920s. Courtesy, Lane County Historical Museum

Beginning in the 1880s, hop picking provided what could be considered an early version of the paid vacation. Hundreds of residents of Eugene, Springfield, Creswell, Goshen, and nearby settlements, as well as Indian families from the Warm Springs Reservation, migrated to the hop fields north and south of Springfield in the late summer.

Most people camped out in tents and enjoyed getting away from their normal chores for a few weeks. Entire families from different social classes came to pick hop flowers off the vines, which were cut from trellises for harvest. It was a once-a-year opportunity for women and children to earn hard cash. In the early part of this century the pay was a penny a pound, and most pickers averaged 100 to 200 pounds a day.

Although it was hot and dusty work, many photos show smiling young men and women wearing suits and pretty dresses. Hop picking was a time of great socializing and romancing. There was music every night, with dancing, singing, games, bonfires, and on Saturday nights a band from town.

Hop pickers carried bags or baskets on a loop around their necks. These containers were emptied into large burlap sacks, which after weighing were hauled to a drying bin. The hops were spread about twenty inches deep on a slatted floor. Workers then built a fire below the bin and placed a pan of sulphur over the flames. The sulphur let off gas, which cured the hop flowers in about twenty-four hours. After curing, the hops were taken to a cooler, a forty-foot-high square tower. There a machine bound them into 200-pound bales. At this point buyers for hops agents, many of them from the Salem area, would contract for the harvest and take delivery.

In the late 1930s, downy hop mildew struck the death blow to local production, but many of Lane County's older residents still recall those days of harvest and fun with considerable nostalgia.

In hop dryers, like these at the Seavy hop yards, sulfur was heated to cure the hop flowers in about twenty-four hours. Courtesy, Lane County Historical Museum

ing have declined in Florence since the beginning of the century, Lane County has one of the world's largest salmon hatcheries. OreAqua, a Springfield subsidiary of Weyerhaeuser Company, releases as many as 20 million young salmon into the Pacific Ocean each year.

As more and more settlers established profitable farms in Lane County, they recognized the benefits of organizing cooperatives. Lane County's first grange was formed in Springfield in 1873. In 1909 all of Lane County's fifty-four granges joined Lane Pomona Grange, a coordinating group that was instrumental in convincing the Eugene City Council to build a farmers' market in 1915.

The first market, located on Park Street at the park blocks, was an immediate success. Its twenty-two stalls grew to eighty stalls by 1925. In 1929 an elegant Spanish-style market opened on the southeast corner of Charnelton and Broadway. The Depression caused serious difficulties, but business picked up slowly in the late 1930s. The market won a national award for excellence during World War II. In the 1950s supermarkets drew business away; the building was finally sold and converted into a Thrifty Drug store in 1959.

The main cooperative produce packer in Lane County is Agripac, Inc. The largest single packer of garden beets in the country, it also packs beans, carrots, sweet corn, and other vegetables and fruit. Agripac began in 1908 when eighty growers pooled their resources as the Eugene Fruit Growers Association to take over a floundering packing plant.

Lane County has had very little mining compared to some other counties in Oregon. Gold was discovered up the McKenzie at Blue River in 1863, and part-time and recreational prospectors still take out small amounts of ore from mountainous areas in the county. However, the major activity occurred in the Bohemia district, southeast of Cottage Grove. There James

"Bohemia" Johnson, reputedly escaping into the hills for having shot an Indian, discovered gold in 1863. Prospectors rushed into the western Cascades to stake out claims. At the turn of the century, mills with sixty stamps were crushing ore, and by 1902 over 2,000 claims had been filed. After a long period of near abandonment, the area has seen some renewed mining efforts in recent years.

The economic history of Lane County entered a bleak period during the 1930s. The Depression caused considerable hardship, though the effects were milder than in some parts of the country. In rural areas people were far more self-sufficient than many city dwellers. Nearly everyone had a garden and a few chickens, and the county's natural abundance provided deer and fish free for the taking. In the cities the lumber mills slowed to a snail's pace. Assistance leagues formed to feed the hungry in soup kitchens and breadlines. Both of Springfield's banks closed, and hundreds of the unemployed traveled on freight trains. After 1932, New Deal programs helped relieve local unemployment. The Public Works Administration built a number of beautifully designed bridges along Oregon's coast that are cherished as landmarks. The Civilian Conservation Corps put many people to work building forest trails and rustic lodges.

Unionization came to Lane County industries in the early 1940s. Although initial recognition of unions was hard-won, the process occurred without the bloodshed seen in other parts of the country. The Booth-Kelly Mill in Springfield was one of the first mills to unionize. Today the International Woodworkers' Association and other lumber-related unions prevail in Lane County. Over the years there have been numerous strikes, especially among the mill workers at Weyerhaeuser, Hines Lumber Company, and Pope and Talbot. The Eugene teachers and the

VACATION SPAS

As early as the 1870s Lane County residents packed up their children for regular summer vacations. The most popular recreational spots in the county were the hot springs to be found up the McKenzie and up the Middle Fork of the Willamette. Visitors from other counties and states also came to these resorts to enjoy the healthful baths and the natural splendor of Lane County.

Hot springs were popular because of their alleged curative powers. Families not only soaked in the hot water to relieve their aches and pains, they also drank the unpleasant-tasting mineral waters for overall good health.

Foley Springs, sixty miles east of Eugene, was purchased by Dr. Abram Foley and opened to the public in 1870. In 1882 Peter Runey bought the property, which is still owned by his descendants. A.G. Walling wrote in his 1884 history of Lane County that the hot water from the two springs was a "specific against all diseases save consumption." He added, "The stream abounds with the finny tribe, while the scenery is unsur-passed. . . . No fewer than fifteen snow-capped peaks are in sight at one time."

Belknap Springs, a few miles away, was first known as Salt Springs because of the high salt content of the water. R.S. Belknap began development in 1870, building a hotel and six cottages. Water from the six hot springs was piped into bathhouses, where visitors had to wait for the water to cool somewhat before enjoying a soak.

Many vacationers took the stagecoach from Eugene to the springs, a trip of about sixteen hours. Fresh horses were required at Walterville, Vida, and Blue River. Travelers ate their noon meal in Leaburg at Aunt Emmy Kennerly's place, which offered chicken, roast, hot bread, potatoes, cake, and fruit pies at less than fifty cents. If travelers preferred not to make the trip in one long day, they could spend the night at Vida or Blue River.

Kitson Springs, up the Willamette past Oakridge, was also developed around 1870. An English bachelor named David Kitson equipped his resort with a wood-lined swimming pool fed by a creek. McCredie Springs, eleven miles from Oakridge, was developed in the early part of this century by John Hardin.

Calapooya Springs at London, Oregon, enjoyed great popularity until the early 1920s, when the failure of the company's bottling business finally forced the closure of the resort. The enterprise began in 1904 when Levi Geer transformed a hop house into a hotel. In addition to a large bathhouse and indoor swimming pool, the resort eventually included a race-track with grandstands. There was a rodeo every Fourth of July. Geer bottled his mineral water as "Cal-A-Poo-Ya Smiling Water" for national distribution, but this venture ran into several problems: notably, transportation and the popularity of the new artificially carbonated soft drinks, as well as Prohibition, which contributed to the demise of many small bottling companies. Nothing is left of the once-thriving development, and over the years even the springs seem to have disappeared.

McKenzie-Willamette Hospital nurses both held lengthy strikes. However, no strike has been marred by violence.

The post-World War II era was a time of unprecedented growth in Lane County. The nationwide boom in housing construction proved a windfall for county residents as the lumber industry flourished. County population, which had grown slowly from 54,493 in 1930 to 69,096 in 1940, surged to 125,776 in 1950. Eugene's population jumped from 20,836 to 35,879 between 1940 and 1950, and Springfield grew remarkably from 3,805 to 10,807.

Recessions in the late 1970s and early 1980s have minimized growth in recent years. To stimulate economic activity that will be compatible with the Metro Plan, both the university and private development organizations are actively courting electronics firms and other "clean" industries in the hope that more of them will build plants and headquarters in Lane County. The making of movies, TV programs, and commercials is always welcomed, and thousands of Lane County residents respond to "cattle calls" for temporary jobs as movie extras.

Tourism is an important industry showing healthy growth. The Eugene/ Springfield Convention and Visitors Bureau, formed in 1980, promotes and coordinates large-scale activities at the Lane County Convention Center and the Eugene Convention Center. In addition to its recreational attractions, the county area offers the world-class Oregon Bach Festival, major sports events such as the Olympic track team trials, and special events like 1984's Olympics Scientific Congress.

Tourists and residents alike enjoy shopping at the Saturday Market and in the Fifth Street Market district. The Fifth Street Public Market is a collection of specialty shops clustered around a courtyard. The building, originally a group of warehouses, has gone through a

couple of successful remodelings, and the market is always crowded with shoppers and coffee drinkers. Across the street several other buildings have been renovated to accommodate the overflow, creating the core of a shopping district.

The Saturday Market originated as a sales outlet for local craftspeople in the late 1960s. Crafts, food, and music still bring plenty of shoppers to the downtown site on a sunny weekend.

Lane County leaders are aware that the county has suffered from limited economic diversification and a dependence on the lumber industry. A number of organizations are dedicated to finding ways to expand the local economy in various directions. Tourism, electronics, and research corporations are three of their brightest hopes for the near future.

Hardworking barn builders pause for a picture in 1904. Courtesy, Lane County Historical Museum

73

THE GOOD LIFE: EDUCATION AND RECREATION

Since the University of Oregon opened its doors in 1876 the entire community has turned to it for cultural and recreational stimulation. Although dancing and theatrics were strictly prohibited during the first years, when students were expected to lead an austere life, a baseball team was organized as early as 1877, and it wasn't long before glee clubs offered sweet sounds to the public. The real campus heroes, however, were the members of the debating teams, the Laurean Society for men and the Eutaxian Society for women.

The professors who instilled the early students with the ideals of classical debate were John M. Johnson, president and Latin scholar, Dr. Thomas Condon, geologist and Congregational minister, and Mark Bailey, a mathematician. That was the entire university staff. The preparatory school affiliated with the university was taught by Mary Spiller and Mary Stone. Dr. Condon, who advocated Darwin's theory of

The University of Oregon won its first football game 24 to 2, defeating Albany College in 1893. Villard Hall, on the left, and Deady Hall, the University's first building, look stark and bare when compared with the lushly wooded and ivy-covered campus of today. Courtesy, Lane County Historical Museum

John M. Johnson, shown here circa 1890, was the first president of the University of Oregon. Courtesy, Dot Dotson's

evolution, was revered by his students and sometimes denigrated by his colleagues, who appreciated neither his scientific beliefs nor his progressive teaching methods.

The university's first building, Deady Hall, was named for Judge Matthew Deady, president of the board of regents. Ten years later, in 1886, the university had a second building, Villard Hall, named for railroad entrepreneur Henry Villard, who donated $10,000 for its construction. The Museum of Art, under construction from 1928 to 1933, is distinguished by a modified Lombardic Romanesque style and brick mosaic facade. The Murray Warner Collection of Oriental Art, a gift from Mrs. Gertrude Bass Warner, is the centerpiece of the perma-

This 1891 faculty meeting included the original teaching staff of the University of Oregon. President John Johnson is seated at the desk; Dr. Thomas Condon is fourth from the right along the wall; and Mark Bailey is first from the left on the benches. Courtesy, University of Oregon Archives

nent collections and features a seventy-inch-tall jade pagoda, considered the largest assembled jade in existence. The Museum of Natural History, as the official state depository, maintains wide-ranging displays of fossils, rocks, and artifacts left by prehistoric Northwest tribes. The museum also provides a showcase for Thomas Condon's extensive fossil collection and the tools he used in his pioneering field work.

University sports events are avidly supported not only by students but by the community at large, especially track and field, basketball, and football. Before these, however, there was the gentle sport of canoeing. The simple outings on the nearby millrace grew by 1911 into lavishly produced fetes with elaborate floats and competition among musical groups.

McArthur Court, seating 10,000 basketball fans, was built in 1926. In 1939 Oregon's fabled Tall Firs earned the national championship. Now called the Ducks, the University of Oregon team draws inveterate fans who are known to have "quack attacks." For football fans Autzen Stadium, built in 1967 across the Willamette River, provides a seating capacity of 41,000. Oregon's football team has gone to the Rose Bowl three times in its history, after the 1957, 1919, and 1916 seasons. In the January 1917 Rose Bowl, quarterback Shy Huntington scored both touchdowns in a 14-0 win over Penn State. Hayward Field, named for William L. Hayward, the university's championship track and field coach from 1903 to 1947, is one of the finest in the country,

among the numerous vocational schools.

Local history is a subject enjoyed by many Lane County residents, whose ancestors began celebrating their pioneer heritage as early as 1883, when the Pioneer Society of Lane County was formed. Original members were the survivors of migrations between 1843 and 1853. Their descendants continue to meet each June for the Pioneer Picnic sponsored by the Lane County Historical Society.

The Eugene Historic Review Board and the Springfield Historical Commission both exist to preserve architectural heritage and promote awareness of the communities' cultural roots. The Lane County Historical Museum, formerly called the Pioneer Museum, houses a fine collection of pioneer artifacts and diaries; visitors note that the stairway and panel-

hosting the Olympic trials in 1972, 1976, and 1980 as well as many other top-ranked meets.

Track and field events are also popular at Lane Community College, which began in 1938 as Eugene Vocational School and became Eugene Technical-Vocational School in 1958. As a publicly supported community college established by voter approval, it held its first classes in 1965. The spectacular campus south of Eugene and Springfield, designed as a complete community for commuting students, was built in 1968-1969. LCC serves students from a 5,000-square-mile area, including all of Lane County and parts of Benton, Linn, and Douglas counties. Classes are also held at LCC centers in downtown Eugene, Cottage Grove, and Florence and in temporary locations throughout the district. College-credit classes are offered on local television channels.

Religious and liberal arts education is available through Northwest Christian College, founded in 1895, and Eugene Bible College, opened in 1925. Eugene Business College, founded in 1901, and a Merritt Davis Business College are

The millrace, built in the 1850s to provide water-power for flour and sawmills, was also used for boating by young couples and students in the early days of the University of Oregon. Courtesy, Lane County Historical Museum

ing from the 1898 courthouse have been integrated into the decor. Often working in support of the museum, the Lane County Historical Society sponsors preservation projects, hosts special events, and publishes the *Lane County Historian,* a periodical devoted to local history.

The Springfield Museum opened in 1981 after years of grass-roots campaigning by local citizens. Use of the beautifully renovated Pacific Power and

Top: *Les Steers, world high-jump record holder from 1940 until 1972, practices a tricky jump as coach Bill Hayward watches.* Right: *Bev Smith, high-scoring women's basketball player, entertained huge crowds in McArthur Court in the early 1980s.* Bottom: *The Tall Firs of 1939 are shown with Governor Charles A. Sprague, holding the trophy, and University of Oregon President Donald M. Erb. Courtesy, University of Oregon Archives*

Light Building is provided by the city council, but all of the staff members are volunteers. The museum features touring exhibits and a permanent collection depicting the history of logging in the region. Other historical museums in Lane County include the Siuslaw Pioneer Museum in Florence, the Oakridge Museum, the Junction City Historical Museum, the Cottage Grove Historical Museum, the Creswell Museum, and the Applegate Pioneer Museum in Crow.

Complementing the area's historical collections is the Willamette Science and Technology Center at Alton Baker Park. Called WISTEC for short, it features entertaining participatory science exhibits.

The building includes the largest planetarium in the Northwest.

When Lane County residents aren't touring museums, they can be found touring out-of-doors by bike, canoe, raft, skis, or on foot. In Eugene and Springfield alone there are fifty developed parks managed by three agencies: the Eugene Parks and Recreation Department, Springfield's Willamalane Parks and Recreation District, and north Eugene's River Road Park District. County and state parks offer additional recreational opportunities, as do civic parks in other towns, such as the beautiful Greenwaters Park in Oakridge.

Miles of jogging trails and bicycle paths attract thousands of users year-round. Eugene bills itself as the running capital of the country, with some justice considering the outstanding track and field program at the university. Many international running stars, including Mary Decker Slaney, Alberto Salazar, and Joaquim Cruz, have trained there or at

THE MCKENZIE DRIFT BOAT: JUST RIGHT FOR WHITE WATER

By the mid-1920s the McKenzie River boats used by guides had taken on a rake—that is, the bottom curved upward fore and aft. Courtesy, Lane County Historical Museum

The McKenzie River has long been known for fine fishing, and since the early part of this century the McKenzie drift boat has been evolving, as river guides have redesigned it for ever greater stability in white water.

Riverman Carey Thomson began rowing for tourists in 1909. He was soon followed into this business by several others, who built lodges all along the McKenzie. Prince Helfrich, who had a degree in geology from the University of Oregon, was one of the leading river guides from the 1920s to the 1960s. In 1931 he was one of the founders of McKenzie River Guides, who at the start of each fishing season sponsored the McKenzie White Water Parade. The tradition continued for thirty-three years, from 1937 to 1970.

By the mid-1920s the boats used by river guides had taken on a rake—that is, the bottom curved upward fore and aft. The sides were higher than before, and experience showed that making the boats shorter and wider—fourteen feet long and four feet wide—enhanced their performance in shallow water. During the 1930s the boats began to have a more pronounced banana-shaped profile, with even higher sides and a wide, high flared stern. Eventually the stern developed into a true "flare-stern" or "square-ender." In 1935 Tom Kaarhus, a commercial boat builder, added more rake to both the stern and the bow, allowing both ends to ride out of water and giving even greater maneuverability.

In the 1940s Woodie Hindman invented a drastically changed drift boat, the prototype of the kind most common today. Hindman turned the flat stern into a point, keeping its height. This pointed end is not the bow, even though it is more pronounced than the true bow. Called the "double-ender," this pointed-stern boat eliminated the chance of stalling in high waves. Several refinements have been made over the years, but the Hindman boat is now the standard McKenzie drift boat, which can be seen on white-water rivers throughout the Northwest.

University of Oregon runners Molly Morton and Kathy Mountain contributed to the school's outstanding tradition in track and field. Courtesy, University of Oregon Archives

Nike, Inc.'s Athletics West facility with coach Dick Brown. The 6.3-kilometer Pre's Trail, circling through Alton Baker Park, is named in memory of Steve Prefontaine, star of the 1972 Olympic trials. Prefontaine held American records at one time or another in almost every long-distance event. His coach at the university and for the 1972 Olympic team,

Rudy Chapa and Alberto Salazar were two of the international running stars who trained at the University of Oregon. Courtesy, University of Oregon Archives

Bill Bowerman, was instrumental in creating Nike, Inc., as well as instigating the popularity of jogging throughout the United States.

The National Academy of Artistic Gymnastics was founded in Eugene in 1973 by Dick Mulvihill and his wife Linda Metheny, a gymnast on the U.S. Olympic team in 1964, 1968, and 1972.

Numerous Olympians, including Julianne McNamara, Tracee Talavera, and Mexico's Tony Pineda, have trained at the academy, which sponsors the national Emerald Cup competition at McArthur Court.

Skiing in the Cascades was enjoyed by a few hardy souls early in the century; recently cross-country skiing has become popular among hikers and joggers of all ages as a sport to enjoy during the winter months. In the summer many of those skiers return to hiking along the Pacific Crest Trail and dozens of other trails, climbing the Three Sisters mountains in eastern Lane County, or enjoying white-water rafting on the McKenzie River.

The Emerald Baseball Club, a farm team of the Kansas City Royals, plays other Northwest League teams at the old Civic Stadium on Willamette Street every summer from June through August. A more unusual sport is a "timberama," or

The campground at Scott Lake in the Cascades offers a spectacular view of the north and middle peaks of the Three Sisters. Courtesy, State of Oregon Photo

Horses graze in a field near Marcola in this painting by M. Goodyear, who was a 1981 winner at the Lane County Fair. Courtesy, Lane County Fair Board

In the back country of the huge Willamette National Forest, Lloyd Van Sickle works with the U. S. Forest Service to maintain trails and shelters. Courtesy, Kevin R. Morris

Opposite page: *A contemporary logging operation is depicted by R.A. Bettencourt. Courtesy, Lane County Fair Board*

Top: *In addition to lumber, products such as particleboard, hardboard, and plywood have become an important part of the timber industry, which accounts for 80 percent of Lane County exports. A 1979 fire at the mill shown here was a serious setback for the economy in Westfir. Courtesy, Don L. Hunter*

Bottom: *An abandoned cabin in the Bohemia district is a reminder of the Oregon gold rush of 1863. Courtesy, State of Oregon Photo*

Top left: *A fall fisherman proudly displays a twenty-five-pound chinook salmon caught in a coastal stream in 1982. Courtesy, Hugh G. Barton*

Top right: *The Row River winds southeast of Cottage Grove amid autumn color. Courtesy, State of Oregon Photo*

Bottom: *Lookout Point Reservoir is surrounded by serene mountain views. Courtesy, State of Oregon Photo*

*A seaside scene by artist
Mel Vincent captures a
mood of Lane County's
coastal area. Courtesy,
Lane County Fair Board*

Opposite page: *A wealth of timber-covered slopes makes Lane County the lumber capital of the United States. Courtesy, Don L. Hunter*

Top: *Wildflowers lend color to Lane County scenery. Courtesy, George Rhoads*

Bottom left: *The forests abound with varieties of edible as well as poisonous mushrooms. Courtesy, George Rhoads*

Bottom right: *McKenzie Pass on State Highway 242 is spectacular in autumn. Courtesy, State of Oregon Photo*

Opposite page: *In eastern Lane County, the Cascade Mountains were home for the Molalla Indians, who hunted deer, elk, and bear in the high meadows and forests. In the west, the lush greenery of the lowlands provided berries and herbs that seasoned the diet of the fish-dependent Siuslaws. Courtesy, Terry Domico/EARTH IMAGES*

The stark beauty of Oregon's sand dunes and the majesty of its rocky coast are admired today by tourists, many coming from thousands of miles away. In another age, this terrain was a barrier to travel, preserving the relative isolation of Lane County's Siuslaw tribe. Courtesy, Terry Domico/ EARTH IMAGES

Top: *The Fern Ridge Reservoir, established after the Flood Control Act was passed in 1936, is now a popular recreation area.* Bottom left: *Children spend vacation days building sand forts on the beach near Cape Perpetua.* Bottom right: *A frosty treat is part of the fun at Junction City's Scandinavian Festival, a family-oriented cultural event that has been held each August since 1960. Courtesy, State of Oregon Photo*

Alton Baker Park, located in Eugene along the Willamette River, was named after a publisher of the Register-Guard newspaper. Courtesy, State of Oregon Photo

Left: *The Butte-to-Butte race is a popular Fourth of July event in Eugene. Courtesy, Hugh G. Barton*

Right: *The annual Scandinavian Festival in Junction City features traditional dancing, food, and costumes. Courtesy, State of Oregon Photo*

Top: *The courtyard of the University of Oregon's Museum of Art is a peaceful spot on campus. Courtesy, State of Oregon Photo*

Bottom left: *Deady Hall, the first building on the University of Oregon campus, was built in 1876 and named for Judge Matthew Deady, president of the board of regents. Courtesy, Don L. Hunter*

Bottom right: *Behind Autzen Stadium at the University of Oregon is the twisting Willamette River. Courtesy, State of Oregon Photo*

Top: *Several bridges, like this one in Florence, were built under New Deal programs during the 1930s and are now cherished as landmarks. Courtesy, Don L. Hunter*

Bottom: *An oldtime train known as the Goose takes visitors along a seventy-mile scenic loop through the hills east of Cottage Grove. Courtesy, State of Oregon Photo*

logging skills competition. Local timbera-mas, generally held in conjunction with outdoor celebrations, offer a chance for men and women to show off their logging expertise and win prizes.

Music has long been a favorite in local entertainment. The Musical McGibeny Family opened an academy in Eugene in 1874 and within two weeks had 100 pupils from a population of 861. The DeMoss Family of Junction City toured perennially with their collection of in-struments; one member of the family de-lighted audiences by playing two cornets at once. Lischen Miller, wife of George M. Miller, and her cousin Catherine Cogswell, a professional actress, initiated local theatrical performances in the 1890s, including productions of Gilbert and Sullivan.

The first touring companies performed in Lane's Opera House, built in 1869 on Eighth Street west of Willamette. Rhine-hart's Hall, opened in 1884 at the corner of Ninth and Oak, was more elegant, but by the 1890s, when it was remodeled and renamed Parker Opera House, its 300 seats were already inadequate. General

Tom Thumb and his company performed there in 1892.

The Eugene Opera House was built in 1903 at Seventh and Willamette. Many of the world's great performers appeared there, including dancer Ruth Saint Denis and John Philip Sousa. In 1922 Calvin Heilig of Portland renamed the theater after himself and began showing films as well as live productions. Today the Hult Center for the Performing Arts is located at the same site.

Not all entertainment took place in-doors. The Lane County Fair began in 1884 and has been growing ever since. The fair provided the kind of entertain-ment approved by the early residents; it was educational as well as pleasurable. The circus, too, was an annual treat, though many an innocent lost money at the circuses and fairs. In 1886 the *Eugene Weekly Register* warned the spectators of Cole's Circus to "look out for the thieves and thugs that will make the visit of the show the opportunity for plying their avocations."

A series of seven pageants held be-tween 1926 and 1950 involved practically the entire population of Eugene and Springfield. The first, entitled "Klatawa—

Far left: *The tiger lily, growing wild in Lane County forests, has been bred and adapted as a garden bloom. Courtesy, George Rhoads*

Left: *Tracee Talavera, member of the 1984 U. S. Olympic team, trained at the National Academy of Artistic Gymnastics in Eugene until 1983. Cour-tesy, National Academy of Artistic Gymnastics*

The Obsidians, a local hiking group, prepare to go on a climb in 1931. Courtesy, Lane County Historical Museum

the Pageant of Transportation," was presented at the Trail to Rail Celebration commemorating the opening of the Natron cutoff, a new route of the Southern Pacific Railroad to California. Performed at Hayward Field on the university campus, and later at the Fairgrounds, the pageants usually continued three days in a row, with 3,000 to 4,000 townspeople participating. Scenery was as long as 400 feet, with various ramps and inclines. Cal Young, a well loved community leader who had been the University of Oregon's first football coach and manager of the Eugene Opera House, often played a stagecoach driver in beaded buckskin. The 1929 pageant, "Sunset Trail," included an epic scene of a wagon train fording the Willamette River, but the most unusual was probably 1934's "Oregon Trail," which somehow featured Mayans and a "Ballet of Many Waters." All but two of the pageants earned a profit. Eventually, heightened audience expectations, requiring special effects

designed in Hollywood, and sharply rising costs brought an end to these spectaculars.

Some of those performing in the pageants were also involved with the Very Little Theater (VLT). Founded in 1929, VLT is considered the oldest continuous community theater in the United States. After performing at the Heilig, the group moved on to a converted store and then to an exhibition hall at the Fairgrounds; in 1950 VLT purchased a lot and built its own theater, designed by a member who was an architect. The theater is entirely self-sufficient and has never relied on grants. The first president, Gerda Brown, continued performing with VLT for over fifty years. Character actor Edgar Buchanan started his career at VLT, as did native son David Ogden Stiers of television's *M.A.S.H.*

University theater developed during the early part of this century, especially under the guidance of Professor Fergus Reddie, who wrote and directed plays.

The Musical McGibeny Family, opening a music school in 1874, enrolled 100 students within two weeks. Courtesy, Lane County Historical Museum

Performances were staged in the Guild Hall Theater, opened in 1915, Villard Hall, and The Braes, a natural amphitheater off Chambers at Eighteenth. Horace Robinson, a nationally known educator, was a leading force for many years and designed a new theater for the university. Built in 1950, it was soon renamed the Robinson Theatre.

The Civic Music Association, later called the Eugene and University Music Association, brought countless national performers to Lane County over decades of activity. In 1944 Helen Hayes and Maurice Evans played to 7,000 spectators in McArthur Court.

The Lane County Auditorium Association began raising money in the 1960s for feasibility studies regarding the construction of a performing arts facility. Ed Ragozzino, who became director of the theater department at Lane Community College, produced ten summer musicals at South Eugene High School, raising $297,092. The culmination of years of effort, the splendid Hult Center for the

Top: *Lischen Miller, on the right, encouraged the development of local theater in the 1890s, which included several productions of Gilbert and Sullivan operettas. Courtesy, Lane County Historical Museum*

Left: *The cast of* Queen Esther *poses in 1910 on the stage of the Eugene Opera House, which became the Heilig Theater in 1922, presenting both legitimate theater and movies. Today the Hult Center for the Performing Arts is located on this site. Courtesy, Lane County Historical Museum*

The DeMoss Family of Junction City was a popular touring musical group in the 1890s. Courtesy, Lane County Historical Museum

Pageants like this one in 1930 were massive local productions involving as many as 3,000 to 4,000 townspeople. Courtesy, Lane County Historical Museum

Performing Arts opened in downtown Eugene in 1982. The center contains two performance halls, the 515-seat Soreng Theater and, reminiscent of European opera houses, the 2,537-seat Silva Concert Hall.

The Hult Center is now the home of various local performance groups, including the Eugene Symphony Orchestra, Eugene Opera, Eugene Ballet Company, Oregon Repertory Theatre, and Oregon Bach Festival. The Eugene Symphony

Orchestra was founded in 1962 by university professor Lawrence Maves, and the Junior Orchestra, for young student musicians, was organized in 1935. The Oregon Bach Festival began as the University of Oregon Summer Festival of Music in 1970; the name was changed in 1981. Each summer the renowned German conductor Helmuth Rilling travels to Eugene for the event, along with numerous distinguished musicians. In 1984 the Oregon Bach Festival performed at the Hollywood Bowl.

Eugene Opera was founded in 1976 by conductor Philip Bayles and mostly local talent. A good training ground for singers breaking into grand opera, the company also hires well known performers from around the country for leading roles.

Eugene Ballet Company was started in 1978 by professional ballet dancers Riley Grannan and Toni Pimble, his English wife. Grannan grew up in Junction City. Having achieved successful careers, both he and his wife wanted to have their own company in the Northwest. Like the opera, Eugene Ballet often hires visiting performers.

Oregon Repertory Theatre began in 1977, growing out of the fledgling Eugene Theatre Company under the guidance of

THE IMAGINATION OF OPAL WHITELEY

Opal Whiteley, child of a humble Cottage Grove logging family, was one of Lane County's most extraordinary, although misguided, talents. In the 1920s she achieved international celebrity, having convinced the world that she was the long-lost daughter of the Duc d'Orleans by his mistress, a princess from India.

In 1919, when she was twenty-two, Opal walked into the office of the *Atlantic Monthly* trying to sell her nature book *The Fairyland Around Us.* In the course of their interview editor Ellery Sedgwick questioned the dark-haired beauty about her childhood. Opal told him a remarkable tale. Asked if she had ever kept a diary, Opal said she had—when she was six and seven years old—but her sister had torn it into pieces. However, she had kept the many pieces throughout the years. Opal sent for them in Los Angeles, where she had been living for the last year and a half, and with the help of the *Atlantic Monthly* staff spent nine months pasting together the crudely printed diary of nearly 140,000 words.

The magazine published the first installment in April 1920, creating tremendous reader interest. In the book, called *The Story of Opal: The Journal of an Understanding Heart,* Opal claimed that after her real parents died, when she was five, she was given to Mrs. Whiteley to replace a dead child. Corroborating her royal birth were the French phrases that filled the diary; Opal had never studied French while living in Oregon. Moreover, all of her childhood plant and animal friends had been given the names of artists and philosophers.

Opal was an overnight sensation. Her book was published in England. Opal persuaded the mother of the late Henri d'Orleans that she was indeed his child. She then traveled to India, where she was accepted as a member of the royal family.

Meanwhile, Opal's family in Cottage Grove endured extreme embarrassment. Mrs. Whiteley had already died, but Opal's sisters changed their last name to Ley and moved from the area. The family was particularly hurt by allegations in the diary that Opal's parents mistreated her, switching her with sticks, making her do all the housework, and ordering her to lie under the bed when she was bad.

In reality, Opal did spend much of her early childhood playing in the woods with wild creatures. Even as a young girl she gave nature lectures and displayed poetic sensibilities. At seventeen she seemed to mesmerize a conference audience of a Christian youth group, which promptly elected her the state president. Although she didn't graduate from high school, her brilliance was evident and she was accepted into the University of Oregon, where she studied for a year and a half.

Little is known of Opal's whereabouts after controversy arose concerning the veracity of her diary. She turned up in London in 1948, ill and mentally impaired. She was placed in an institution, where she remained for many years. According to Opal's family, the story of her royal heritage was the product of an overactive imagination. Although no one has been able to disprove that she wrote her diary as a child, it is considered more likely that she wrote it while living in Los Angeles. In any case, *The Story of Opal* remains an entertaining creation, with lovely and loving descriptions of a child's forest friends.

Die Fledermaus was performed in 1982 by Eugene Opera. The company was first organized in 1976 by conductor Philip Bayles, who received a Eugene Arts and Letters award in 1984 for his outstanding work.

The town turned out to view the Liberty Bell when it arrived on tour one sunny July afternoon in 1915. Courtesy, Lane County Historical Museum

actress Randi Douglas. From 1978 to 1985 David Lunney served as artistic director, keeping the theater alive through times of financial difficulty and bringing it onto solid ground with general manager Steve Caffery. Dedicated to new and classic American plays, Oregon Repertory Theatre has presented several world premieres.

Jane Van Boskirk, founder of a small touring theater company based in Eugene, Northwest Touring Theatre, has been performing *The Northwest Woman* and other plays throughout Oregon, Washington, and Idaho since 1980.

Lane County is the home of several prominent authors, including novelist Ken Kesey; science fiction writers Kate Wilhelm, Damon Knight, John Varley, and Geoffrey Simmons; renowned short story writer Kay Boyle; and Barry Lopez, whose reflections on nature defy categorizing. Lane County's best known nineteenth-century writers were Joaquin Miller and Samuel L. Simpson, considered Oregon's poet laureate and called the "Poet of the Willamette." Sophus K. Winther, who grew up in Danebo, west of Eugene, is recognized for two works: a fictional trilogy on Danish immigration to America and a novel, *Beyond the Garden Gate,* set in Eugene in the 1930s.

In the field of music, several performers and groups originating in Lane County have gained national recognition, among them the Jazz Minors, talented young musicians who perform for the Walt Disney Company. Mason Williams of Oakridge is a Grammy-winning guitarist and composer. Alan Kaye, from Eugene, sings leading roles for various opera companies.

In fine arts, the Lane County tradition extends from such painters as David McCosh, Alfred Schroff, and Lance Hart to contemporary artists Jan Zach, La Verne Krause, and Vernon Witham. Lane County is known throughout the West as a major center for craftspeople, especially weavers, jewelry makers, ceramicists, and clothing designers.

Annual festivals are part of the good life enjoyed in Lane County. Springfield hosts the Springfest, Fourth of July Celebration, Broiler Festival, and Octoberfest. Eugene pulls out all the stops for Saint Patrick's Day, the Emerald Empire Roundup, the Butte to Butte Run on the Fourth of July, and the Eugene Celebration in September. Thousands of visitors each year attend these and other special events described in the following chapter, which is devoted to Lane County communities.

LANE COUNTY COMMUNITIES

Eugene Skinner wanted to build a city, and he made a good choice when he selected his Donation Land claim on *Ya-po-ah* butte overlooking the Willamette River. This land became a natural crossroads for homesteaders and miners alike. Over half of the county's residents now live in the adjoining cities of Eugene and Springfield, while no other town has a population of even 10,000. Despite new shopping centers and modern bank buildings, most of Lane County's towns and villages maintain a rural nineteenth-century ambience. Because of the geographical variety of the county, the towns have their own distinctive character.

The Lane County coastal area began to develop after an act of Congress in 1875 opened a major part of the Siletz Indian Reservation for white settlement. Settlers came first to the mouth of the Siuslaw River, where the town of Florence grew, and gradually ventured farther up the coast. Access through the Coast Range

The brilliantly white Heceta Head Lighthouse dates back to 1893. This often-photographed feature of Lane County scenery is shown here in 1915. Courtesy, Lane County Historical Museum

Because of the geographical variety across the area, from the Pacific Ocean on the west to the Cascade Mountains on the east, Lane County communities have their own distinctive character.

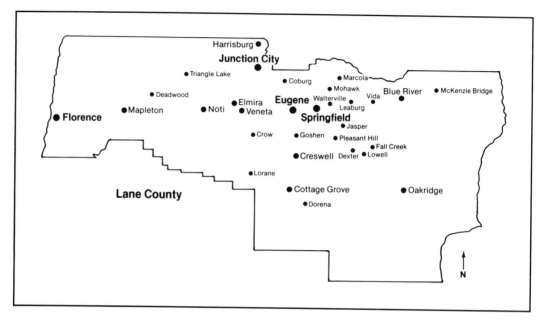

George M. Miller, active in real estate in the 1890s, developed the Fairmount area in Eugene and did much to promote the coastal area. Courtesy, Lane County Historical Museum

from the Willamette Valley was extremely difficult for many years. In the 1890s George M. Miller of Eugene avidly promoted the construction of a "New York to Florence Highway." It was an idea whose time hadn't come, and even the Eugene to Florence highway wasn't completely paved until 1959. Nevertheless Miller's promotions did much to develop the coastal area.

Florence. The town of Florence was founded in 1876 when Duncan and Company built a fish cannery and A.J. Moody opened a store. Steamers transported cargoes of canned salmon and lumber directly to California. In later years canning and fishing gave way, and tourism became important to the area.

In the 1970s shopkeepers and craftspersons in Florence began an exceptionally successful revitalization campaign. A three-block section of Bay Street along the Siuslaw waterfront, once the center of town, was beautifully refurbished and today houses a number of prosperous shops and restaurants. The Kyle Building from 1901 is a centerpiece of Bay Street renovation, and the nearby Kennedy-Johnson house, built in 1892, serves as a bed and breakfast establishment. A mile and a half upriver from Florence the abandoned Bennedict house, built in 1906, is said to have been the inspiration for the Stamper house in Ken Kesey's novel *Sometimes a Great Notion.*

Florence is the scene of a Rhododendron Festival each May, when thousands of pink blossoms decorate the landscape. A more unusual flower, the insect-eating cobra lily, can be seen five miles north of Florence at the Darlingtonia Botanical

Elizabeth Romane took this photo of the quaint community of Mapleton in 1910. Courtesy, Lane County Historical Museum

Wayside, an eighteen-acre state preserve. A few miles farther north are the Sea Lion Caves, long a popular tourist attraction. Sea lions live at the base of the rocky coastal cliff year-round, taking refuge in the caves during stormy weather. Just beyond the caves is Heceta Head, named for Spanish sea captain Bruno Heceta, who sailed along the coast in 1775. Heceta Head is the site of a much-photographed lighthouse, built in 1893. The assistant lighthouse keepers' house, a Queen Anne-style duplex nearby, is said by many to be haunted.

Just south of Florence is the village of Glenada, which incorporated in 1912 and disincorporated in 1922, after its sawmills burned. Dunes City and Siltcoos, a few miles farther south, are both located on Siltcoos Lake. Tiernan, a tiny settlement between Florence and Mapleton, was established in 1919 for local mill workers. The post office closed in 1970, and the few remaining businesses departed when the highway was widened. The drawbridge at nearby Cushman was built in 1915, and for years it was opened whenever a sailing schooner needed to go up-river to Mapleton.

Mapleton. On the Siuslaw River, Mapleton was first settled in 1876 by

This marching band calls attention to the Rhododendron Festival of 1912 in Florence. The festival is held each May. Courtesy, Lane County Historical Museum

Zolmon and Onslo Young and their families. Two years later they were joined by Frank and Elizabeth Knowles. In 1886 the Obadiah Bean family built a hotel with a post office. Mrs. Bean wanted to call the post office Maple Leaf, because there were seventeen maple trees in front of the hotel, but the government decided that name was too long and shortened it to Mapleton. Also in 1886 Emma Bean became the town's first schoolteacher. In the 1890s construction began on an unusual fish hatchery, probably the only one in the world with a dance hall on the second floor.

Mapleton, with 100 inches of rain each

year, has often suffered from floods and mudslides, the worst taking place in 1890 and 1965. Fishing, farming, and logging have always been the mainstays of the local economy.

Many of Mapleton's old wooden buildings have been renovated by members of the Alpha Farm commune, located thirteen miles away in the isolated settlement of Deadwood. Deadwood has become a haven for a small colony of artists and craftspersons wanting to get away from it all. However, resident Mary Lou Goertzen has become nationally known for her delicate floral designs on fine china.

The valleys west of Eugene are dotted with numerous "century farms" (owned by the same family for 100 years) and small communities that grew around a country store, a grange hall, or a church. The Farmer Hale house, west of Noti, was built in 1909 and served as a stagecoach stop. In the Noti and Walton area the most memorable building is the bright blue Noti Grade School, built in 1927. In the 1920s Forcia and Larsen Company established a sawmill at Noti, which is now one of the last of the Coast Range lumber towns.

Elmira. Elmira was first settled around 1851 by Isaac and Julia Ann Duckworth. A mill was built in 1881, and in 1892 W.T. and Martha Kayser added a combined store, post office, and residence. There was also a busy stagecoach stop, the Elmira Hotel, for tourists traveling to and from the coast. In 1909 the high school was organized. Today Elmira is becoming known for its vineyards and winemaking. Triangle Lake nearby was a popular weekend destination for Eugene residents during the 1920s.

Veneta. Part of the Applegate Trail and some of Lane County's oldest farms were claimed when the Fern Ridge Reservoir was built in 1941, including those of Benjamin Richardson, Joel C. Inman, and John Lasater. Today the reservoir, home of the Eugene Yacht Club, provides the most popular freshwater sailing in the county. Nearby Veneta, a growing commuter community, was founded in 1912 by Edmund Hunter and Charles Dunham. The town began with railroad construction and a few stores; the post office was added in 1914 with Ross Elliott as postmaster. The town enjoyed a lumber boom in the 1920s until the stock market crash. Like many small cities, Veneta is now actively pursuing economic

Turn-of-the-century Elmira was a busy stop for tourists traveling to and from the coast. Courtesy, Lane County Historical Museum

The first graduating class of Elmira Union High School posed for a commemorative photo in 1914. Courtesy, Lane County Historical Museum

diversification. Near Veneta the Oregon Country Fair, a mecca for Northwest craftspeople and entertainers, is held each summer.

Junction City. By the 1850s many fine farms had been developed in the area northwest of Eugene, but Junction City didn't come into existence until 1871, when the Oregon and California Railroad purchased Donation Land claims from T.A. Milliorn, L.D. Gilbert, and G.H. McQueen for a railroad junction. The small town flourished, and within a year there were stores, a hotel, a saloon, a blacksmith shop, a warehouse, a school, and several other buildings. In 1872 the town was incorporated.

In 1878 a devastating series of fires destroyed nearly all of the buildings and many thousands of dollars' worth of property. Ironically, the city council had voted the year before to contribute $500 toward a fire engine if residents would donate an equal amount. The residents refused. After the fires no insurance company would risk insuring property in Junction City for a whole year.

At the turn of the century numerous Danish immigrants moved to the area,

purchasing forty- to sixty-acre all-purpose farms. Many prospered and built substantial farmhouses along Dane Lane. The early Danish settlers, who practiced agriculture, were soon joined by Norwegian and Swedish immigrants, who helped develop the local lumber industry. In 1902 A.C. Nielsen, a real estate dealer from Minnesota, established the Danish Lutheran Church, which served as a community center. Until 1951 services were held in both Danish and English.

Junction City today is known throughout the Northwest as the scene of the

A blacksmith shop, like this one photographed circa 1910, was among the first establishments in the budding town of Junction City. Courtesy, Lane County Historical Museum

Industrious Scandinavian immigrants established all-purpose farms near Junction City at the turn of the century. Courtesy, Lane County Historical Museum

Company E, 4th Infantry Band, stands in Cottage Grove's Main Street in 1907. Main Street has preserved its old-fashioned look. Courtesy, Lane County Historical Museum

colorful four-day Scandinavian Festival, held each August since 1960. During the festival, downtown streets are blocked off to allow as many as 90,000 visitors to roam among Scandinavian-style booths. The idea for the first festival came from Dr. Gale Fletchall, who wanted to bring people to the city for a family-oriented cultural event. Scandinavian songs, dances, costumes, and food are highlighted, as well as crafts and readings from works of Scandinavian authors.

Cottage Grove. Historian A.G. Walling wrote in 1884 that Cottage Grove "bears the appearance of thrift and prosperity." Some of the stores from that era still adorn its old-fashioned Main Street, complementing a number of fine Queen Anne-style homes. Located south of Eugene, Cottage Grove was first settled in 1848. The earliest school, a log cabin, was built in 1853, and Charles Samuels opened the first store in 1857. Although the surrounding land was of a lesser quality than farther north in the Willamette Valley, it was good enough for raising profitable wheat crops and for grazing livestock. Cottage Grove came into its own as one of the earliest lumber centers in Lane County, and the industry is still important, with Weyerhaeuser and Bohemia mills, in this city of 7,000 residents.

In the 1850s many of the settlers who had left their farms to join the Gold Rush in California returned and continued to search for gold locally. They found it in the nearby Calapooya Mountains: 2,000 mines had been located in the Bohemia Mining district by the 1890s. Today the city remembers its mining heritage with Bohemia Days each July. Featured events include an old-time fiddlers' festival, a rodeo, parades, an ugly dog contest, historic-home and museum tours, and an excursion to the mining district aboard an antique train known as the Goose. This railway line, along a mountainous seventy-mile loop, is one of the city's most popular and nostalgic attractions. Begun in 1902, it is now one of America's last short-line scenic railways. The Goose is hauled by a diesel engine on weekdays and on weekends by a 1915 Baldwin steam locomotive.

The train passes by Dorena Lake, created in 1947 as a combined recreational and flood-control project; Cottage Grove Reservoir is available for the same purpose. Several movies and television commercials have been filmed in the area, including *Animal House,* which used Cottage Grove's Main Street for its parade scenes.

Creswell. Halfway between Eugene and Cottage Grove, Creswell began in the 1850s as the original location of the Cottage Grove post office. The post office was soon moved farther south. The settlement at Creswell remained and was named for Postmaster General A.J. Creswell. It wasn't until 1872 that J.T. Gilfry erected the first local store. In 1878 John Trunnell built a three-story mill for $10,000. A fire claimed much of the town in 1882, but residents rebuilt on a more substantial scale. The town's first school building, erected in 1875, survived the fire and is now the Creswell Civic Improvement Club and Library. The Methodist Episcopal Church, built in 1889, serves as the Creswell Historical Museum. The town incorporated in 1909.

In 1908 the Bohrnstedt Orchard Company, representing Easterners owning 2,000 acres of apple orchards, participated in the founding of the Creswell Fruit Growers' Bank. The Creswell Cannery opened around 1913. Today Willamette Poultry is a major employer in the area, as is the Emerald Valley Inn, which offers a resort, golf course, and convention center. The Creswell Air Fair, featuring stunts with antique airplanes, attracts as many as 15,000 visitors in the summer.

Goshen. Bordered by hills and water, tiny Goshen began as a farming community and never grew into a real town. The first settlers in Goshen, south of Eugene, were Milton Riggs and his brother Rufus, who arrived around 1850. Their brother Washington and his wife Matilda moved nearby in the following year; their daughter Ann Clarinda was probably the first white child born in the area. Other early families included Silas and Sarah Severn and John Jacob and Elizabeth Hampton, whose daughter Eliza had married Milton Riggs. The Goshen post office was established in 1874, and the settlement gained a depot on the Oregon and California Railroad in the late 1870s. The farms around Goshen were noted for hop growing and livestock.

The Stone house is one of many Queen Anne-style houses remaining in Cottage Grove. Courtesy, Lane County Historical Museum

In addition to a busy creamery, Creswell prospered in the early 1900s by the Creswell Fruit Growers' Bank and the Creswell Cannery. Courtesy, Lane County Historical Museum

Dorena. Early settlers in the Dorena area included Greenbury Van Shoiack, John Harms, Gordon McCauley, James R. Hobson, and Mark Calvert, all of whom took up Donation Land claims in 1853. The post office, established in 1899, was named for two girls, Dora Burnette and Rena Martin. This area on the Row River east of Cottage Grove was less fertile than the Willamette Valley, so when gold was discovered at Bohemia, a number of Dorena residents turned to prospecting, road building, and railroad building. The Oregon and South Eastern Railroad, known as "Old Slow and Easy," came through in 1902-1903, and excursion trains began running to Wildwood Falls.

Logging developed in conjunction with the railroad. Soon there were twenty-three mills on the Row River, as well as many others in the area. Lumbermen active locally included J.I. Jones, John Q. Doud, Jasper Patten, and the Doolittle family. In spite of mining and lumber activity, farming and stock raising continued to dominate the local economy through the 1940s. The townsite was relocated several miles upriver when construction on the Dorena Reservoir began in 1941. Some of the buildings and homes were moved, others were burned. One

hundred families resettled in the new town, as roads, railroads, and water lines were rerouted. This town has retained the rural atmosphere of old Dorena.

Lorane. A tiny settlement west of Cottage Grove, Lorane is situated on one of the oldest roads in the state, originally a north-south Indian trail improved by Hudson's Bay Company trappers in the 1820s. In 1846 Jesse and Lindsay Applegate and Captain Levi Scott turned the trail into a rough wagon road for immigrants entering the territory from the south. In 1857 Philip Sheridan built the West Side Territorial Road to facilitate movement of troops.

Near Lorane, Darius Cartwright built the Mountain House Hotel, one of the first stagecoach inns. As the northern terminus of the telegraph line from California, this station was the first in Lane County to receive news of Lincoln's assassination. This historic house was demolished in the late 1960s. Several turn-of-the-century buildings are still in use, including the grange, the general store, and the Christian Church.

Crow. The small community of Crow is believed to be named for Andrew Jackson Crow, an 1852 settler. The Applegate Pioneer Museum, founded by Zelda Harwood, houses local artifacts pertaining to the Applegate Trail and early settlers in the area. The museum is located in the old Pine Grove School, donated by the Spencer Creek Lutheran Church for that purpose.

Pleasant Hill. In the summer of 1846 Elijah Bristow, the first settler in the Willamette Valley, staked his claim and called it Pleasant Hill. His property became the site for the first schoolhouse and the first church in Lane County. Soon other settlers joined him, and Pleasant Hill developed into a small farming community, which it remains to this day. Bristow's son, William W. Bristow, built a fine home in 1863 that stands out as one of Lane County's best examples of the Gothic Revival style. The Taylor Barn was built around 1870, and the Church of Christ is a 1913 landmark. Pleasant Hill is the home of novelist Ken Kesey.

Jasper. The Middle Fork of the Willamette was settled in 1847-1848 by Cornelius and Sephronia Hills. Their son Jasper, born in 1859, was the first male white child born in the region. About 1880 the small settlement was named after him at the suggestion of D.C. Wallace, another pioneer. The first school was built in 1876, with Ada Walton as teacher. In 1880 James Keeney opened a general store, adding a post office in 1884. Adam Horn, a farmer, started the area's first Evergreen blackberries, which had been sent out from the East. People soon came from all over the Willamette Valley to get starters from him. The rampant blackberries are now considered a nuisance by many.

Fall Creek. Many Fall Creek pioneers came west in 1853 with the Lost Wagon Train as emigrants from the British Isles. George H. Penland, John Fothergill, Richard W. Lewis, William Drinkwater, and Joseph Drinkwater established land claims in 1853 and 1854. John Stewart of Scotland settled nearby. In the 1880s stock raising was the major source of in-

come in the area, but near the turn of the century logging became preeminent.

Both the Fall Creek and Winberry ranger stations were established in 1907. During the 1930s the Civilian Conservation Corps upgraded ranger station facilities, built trails, and developed recreational camps. Less productive was the mining exploration that took place during the 1930s: no major gold strikes. The Fall Creek Reservoir was completed in 1965.

Lowell. The farmland in the Lowell area was not as attractive to the first settlers as that around Pleasant Hill. Settlement came partly as a result of exploration up the Middle Fork of the Willamette in search of a pass through the mountains. A few settlers took up homesteads in the 1850s, and in 1865 the Oregon Central Military Road came through.

In 1874 Amos D. Hyland, a farmer near Junction City, purchased 2,450 acres in the area and named the property for Lowell, Maine, a former residence. The local post office, established in 1880 with C.E. Byers as postmaster, was at first named Cannon but changed to Lowell in 1883. The prominent Hyland family took

Jasper Hills, standing left of Clyde Huntly and George Kelly on a hunting trip in 1912, was the first male white child born in the area of Jasper, which was named for him. Courtesy, Lane County Historical Museum

In 1923 a large mill and company town were built by George Kelly in Westfir. Courtesy, Lane County Historical Museum

up general farming, hop growing, livestock, and storekeeping. The store, operated by son-in-law Albert E. McFarland, was the major supplier for the region, provisioning families scattered far up the Middle Fork.

In the twentieth century logging provided an additional source of income, and between 1947 and 1961 the construction of the contiguous Dexter and Lookout Point reservoirs offered employment to many residents. Approximately 150 landowners relinquished hundreds and in some cases thousands of acres. Many homes were relocated before the lower edges of Lowell were covered by water. However, the railroad and state highway were moved to the opposite bank of the reservoir, cutting Lowell off from most potential growth.

Dexter. Samuel Handsaker's store was the early center of activity as Dexter developed on the south bank of the Middle Fork of the Willamette. In 1872 Handsaker became postmaster for Butte Disappointment, which was renamed Dexter in 1875. Farming and eventually timber provided a modest living for the handful of residents. Dexter and Lookout Point reservoirs, completed in 1961, attract weekend sailors and water skiers.

Oakridge. Located up the Middle Fork of the Willamette River, Oakridge calls itself the "Tree Planting Center of the World." The scene of a fall Tree Planting Festival since 1953, Oakridge is the center of operations for planting 500,000 seedlings per year.

The Oakridge area was settled after the Lost Wagon Train and subsequent wagon trains began traveling the route through the Willamette Pass. James and Richard Sanford were among the first who came to the area in 1860. The earliest settlement, called Big Prairie, soon became known as Hazeldell or Hazeldale. By 1870 the Oregon Central Military Road was completed, connecting the Willamette Valley with Fort Boise in Idaho. The

road brought more settlers to Oakridge, including David Kitson, an Englishman who developed nearby Kitson Hot Springs.

In 1909 construction began on a new railroad that would shorten the Eugene to California route. The line reached Oakridge in 1912, when the town changed its name from Hazeldell. Oakridge became a railroad town, operating a roundhouse and a garage stall for engines. Partly because of the availability of transportation, the Fish and Game Commission established a fish hatchery in the Oakridge area in 1917.

In 1923, George Kelly, a former owner of the Booth-Kelly Lumber Company, built the first large mill and company town at the nearby settlement of Westfir. In 1944 Hines Lumber Company purchased the mill for $2 million, operating it until production ceased in 1978. With the opening of the Pope and Talbot mill in 1948, Oakridge's population grew to approximately 4,000.

The town has always been a starting point for hunting and fishing expeditions to the nearby mountains and a center for extensive U.S. Forest Service activity. The thriving Willamette Pass Ski Area has been operating since the 1940s for downhill skiers, and numerous cross-country trails attract skiers of all ages. Also nearby are the massive Salt Creek

Falls, the second highest waterfall in Oregon, and Waldo Lake, one of the state's largest lakes. Dozens of lakes dot the area. The Oakridge Chamber of Commerce now promotes the town as a recreational and retirement center.

Coburg. Six miles north of Eugene, the Coburg area was first settled in 1847 by Jacob Spores and John Diamond. Many of Coburg's earliest buildings are still in use. The home of Isaac Van Duyn, begun in 1848, is probably the oldest building in Lane County. A later Van Duyn home, built in 1877, is now the Coburg Inn. Another early settler was Hulins Miller, father of Joaquin and George M. Miller.

Coburg was named for a prize stallion imported from Coburg, Germany, by Charles Payne, the first blacksmith. The town was incorporated in 1907, the same year that local businessmen invited eight Norwegian artisans to start a glass factory. The factory was unsuccessful, but the period between 1898 and 1915 could be considered Coburg's golden years. Two sawmills, including a Booth-Kelly mill, offered good jobs for a rapidly growing population. Four daily trains ran between Coburg and Eugene, as did public coaches. Coburg has endured severe flooding of the McKenzie River but retains its bucolic nineteenth-century atmosphere.

"I come to the McKenzie River for a brainwashing and to refresh my soul," former President Herbert Hoover told a reporter in 1956. From 1932 to 1958 he visited the McKenzie two or three times a year, usually staying at Holiday Farm Resort in Rainbow. Many other statesmen and celebrities have found respite on the McKenzie, which has drawn thousands of tourists since the 1870s.

Walterville. Springfield is known as the "Gateway to the McKenzie," but Walterville is the first of a string of small settlements along the river between Springfield and McKenzie Pass in the Cascade Mountains. George Millican, an early settler, named Walterville in 1862 for his son, the first white child born in the area. In addition to serving as postmaster, George Millican was instrumental in developing a road along the McKenzie. In 1888 he donated property for the Walterville School. The Eugene Water and Electric Board built a power plant at Walterville in 1910.

Deerhorn, a few miles farther east, had sparse early settlement but did boast a school. Today it is a community of commuters, who enjoy fishing and golf in their spare time.

Leaburg. Leaburg takes its name from the first postmaster, Leander Cruzan. The post office, established in 1877, was preceded by the first school, built in 1873. In the earliest days of tourism the stagecoaches stopped in Leaburg for the noon meal at Jim and Emmy Kennerly's house. The McKenzie Salmon Hatchery, established in 1910-1911, is one of the oldest enterprises on the river.

Benjamin Franklin Finn, who claimed to be the Huckleberry Finn made famous by Mark Twain, moved his family from Missouri to the Leaburg area in 1871. He worked as a bricklayer and manufactured

The Van Duyn family, early settlers in Coburg, built a house in 1848 that stands today as probably the oldest structure in Lane County. This store was a busy place at the turn of the century. Courtesy, Lane County Historical Museum

Top: *Blue River was a supply center for this 1904 miner and the others who tried their luck prospecting for gold in the Cascades. Courtesy, Lane County Historical Museum*

Bottom: *The settlement of Mohawk, originally called Donna, was a busy lumber depot early in the century. Courtesy, Lane County Historical Museum*

whiskey and turpentine. He and his sons also sold deer hams in Eugene for six cents a pound.

Vida. Frank Pepiot and his family, French Canadians, moved to the Vida area in 1868 and Theron Thomson brought his family to nearby Goodpasture the following year. The first school was held in the Thomson home in 1872. The area was originally called Gate Creek, but Frank Pepiot, establishing a post office in 1898, changed the name to Vida, for his daughter. Vida had a small hotel run by Ben Minney and a sports-

man's lodge built by Carey Thomson. His sons built the larger Thomson Lodge around 1911, catering to fishermen for many years.

Blue River. Blue River was named in 1863, when gold was discovered in the area. The post office was established near the mouth of Blue River, where it flows into the McKenzie, in 1886 with John M. Davis as postmaster. Samuel Sparks founded the town of Blue River, and his son Felix built the first sawmill. The town became the supply center for vigorous mining activity in the rugged surrounding terrain, especially after the 1887 discovery of the Lucky Boy Mine. Most of the residents were men. Robenia Sparks, who ran a stagecoach inn with her husband Samuel, reported that at one time she didn't see another woman for three months. By 1912, as the high-grade ore ran out, mining activity gave way to fishing and tourism. Logging has been important since the 1940s, and construction workers found employment building dams in the 1950s and 1960s.

McKenzie Bridge. John Templeton Craig came in the 1860s to the McKenzie Bridge area, which was at first called Strawberry Prairie for the profusion of wild strawberries growing there. Craig built a crude temporary bridge over the river, charging a toll to cross. Theron Thomson later built a more substantial bridge in the same spot, and his son Carey constructed an additional bridge in 1890. The first store at McKenzie Bridge was operated by Lew Powers.

When gold was discovered in Idaho in the 1860s, it became important to have an improved road through the McKenzie Pass. The existing road climbed treacherous grades through lava beds that tore the animals' hooves and shredded the travelers' shoes. John Craig played a major role in locating and building the new road, on which there was a toll until 1898. Craig carried mail across the pass through all weather until he died in a terrible blizzard at the end of 1877.

The U.S. Bureau of Public Roads built the McKenzie Pass Highway in 1925. This steep, winding road is now a scenic route kept open only during the summer months; during the rest of the year, covered by deep snowdrifts, it is favored by experienced cross-country skiers. In the 1930s the Civilian Conservation Corps built sections of the Skyline Trail, which became the Pacific Crest National Scenic Trail in 1968, as well as campgrounds, picnic areas, bridges, and watch towers.

Aside from several covered bridges, probably the most famous landmark at McKenzie Bridge is the Log Cabin Inn. The original structure, from 1886, was destroyed by fire in 1906. Rebuilt the following year as a stagecoach stop, the spacious two-story log cabin continues to offer hospitality to travelers from around the world. A few miles beyond McKenzie Bridge are Foley Hot Springs and Belknap Hot Springs, popular holiday spots since the 1870s.

The Mohawk Valley. Lane County's Mohawk River was probably named for the Mohawk River in New York. The valley through which it runs, located northeast of Springfield, attracted settlers first with its rich pasturelands and later with its thick stands of timber. Mary and Columbus (known as Lum) Cole built the first mill in Marcola in the 1850s. The town was first called Isabel, for the wife of Elisha Applegate, and the post office was established in that name in 1876. But there were several Oregon towns named Isabel, and when Lum Cole became postmaster, he renamed it Marcola for his wife.

By 1900 the entire valley was a bustling scene of logging activity. The Southern Pacific Railroad was completed in 1902, with two passenger trains daily to Eugene. The settlement of Mohawk, first called Donna for resident Donna Jackson, was a thriving logging depot in the early 1900s; it is now a small rural center.

Two towns in the Mohawk Valley, once booming with logging activity, have almost disappeared in modern times. Mabel, named for resident Maud Mabel Drury, had the first mill in the region. Wendling was a company town built at the turn of the century by Booth-Kelly. In 1946, when its Mohawk Valley timber lands had been virtually depleted, the Booth-Kelly logging camps were dismantled or burned down. Today nothing but foundations remain at the once lively townsites of Wendling and Mabel. Mohawk Valley residents continue to farm and raise stock, and many work in Springfield or Eugene.

The only comprehensive history of Lane County previous to this one was published in 1884. The themes of growth, change, and variety, as delineated by Dr. Richard M. Brown in his foreword, will become increasingly evident in the next hundred years. Lane Countians, like many Americans, will find new ways of making a living and new ways of enjoying their leisure time. But the physical beauty of Lane County will not diminish, because residents will continue to protect that beauty, as well as the bounty of our land and waters. Our appreciation of these treasures, equally cherished by our ancestors, is abiding and will be passed on to future generations.

The McKenzie Pass Highway was kept open during the winter in the late 1920s. Hardy sightseers passed between deep snowbanks on their trip to the top. Courtesy, Lane County Historical Museum

PARTNERS IN PROGRESS

In 1846, when Eugene F. Skinner stood atop the butte that now bears his name and decided he was home, he was mapping a plan not only for his own family's future but also was unknowingly establishing the framework for a community that would grow and thrive and be both home and workplace to the many thousands who would choose to live in this lovely timber-rich area at the head of the Willamette Valley.

Over the mountains and across the plains the settlers have come. In wagons on the Oregon Trail, in rickety Fords bouncing out of the Dust Bowl, and in U-Haul vans and jet airplanes, new residents have brought their hopes, their dreams, and their worldly possessions to Eugene, Springfield, Coburg, Veneta, Cottage Grove, Creswell, Junction City, Florence, and the myriad small communities that comprise the vast expanse that is Lane County, stretching from the mountains to the sea.

Commerce and livability combined to draw adventurous young men and women as well as entire families to the area. And, once here, they created the institutions that improved life and drew yet others—the university, the hospitals, the community college, and the businesses that offered jobs, services, and products.

The early settlers came to work the land—as farmers or as lumberjacks and mill workers—and the later immigrants came for the wide-open spaces and the clean air unfouled by industrial pollution. For 100 years industry meant timber in Lane County, and that industry spawned other businesses, which in turn brought more people.

Eugene, now the second-largest city in the state, became a home to both the major state university and the county's community college; Springfield sprouted processing plants; family farms turned into commercial enterprises; and shopping centers sprang up in the valley as motels and restaurants appeared along the coast to tempt the tourist traffic.

By the end of the 1970s, however, the national economic slump was beginning to catch up with Lane County. The mills slowed down or closed, the developers stopped building, even the university saw a drop in student enrollment.

Now community leaders are looking to a future based on more than timber and scenic backroads. They are courting high-technology industry, and the area is seeing some progress in that field.

The coastal ports are looking west, hoping to take advantage of Oregon's Pacific Rim status to forge new ties with Japan and China. The farmers and the manufacturers, too, are looking abroad and developing trade agreements that will take Lane County products not only to the Far East but also to Latin America and Australia.

The organizations whose stories are detailed on the following pages have chosen to support this important literary and civic project. They illustrate the variety of ways in which individuals and their businesses have contributed to the area's growth and development. The civic involvement of Lane County's businesses, institutions of learning, and local government, in cooperation with its citizens, has made the community an excellent place to live and work.

CHAPTER VIII

*A harvest of wheat, seen against a horizon of timber-
land, and the arrival of the regular stagecoach at Mountain House, near Lorane, illustrated the beginnings of
Lane County commerce in A.G. Walling's 1884 history.
Courtesy, Lane County Historical Museum*

LANE COUNTY HISTORICAL SOCIETY

Although the first official meeting of what is today the Lane County Historical Society was held in 1954, the organization traces its roots to the 1880s and the Lane County Pioneer Association, an informal group of pioneers and their descendants who met annually for a picnic and to elect officers. That first loosely structured group, however, did little in the way of actually maintaining historical artifacts or county data. Interest in preserving pioneer relics and information on the region's settlers was sparked with the first three "Oregon Trail" pageants, staged with the help of the association in 1926, 1929, and 1934.

The last pageant was held in 1950, but that did not end interest in an organized approach to preserving local history. A warehouse had been built at the fairgrounds to house memorabilia Cal Young had collected during the pageants. Long after the pageants ended, the older group of Pioneer Association members continued to meet for the annual picnic on the Saturday nearest the birthday of Young, who had been a county commissioner and the University of Oregon's first football coach.

The group was reorganized in 1954 as the Lane County Pioneer-Historical Society, with 167 members of pioneer heritage. At that first meeting, called by Josephine Harpham, Merle Moore was elected president of the society. Moore was instructed by the group to begin collecting pictures of standing buildings and copies of those already destroyed—a project that re-

These statues in honor of the Pioneer Mother and the Pioneer Father are located on the University of Oregon campus in Eugene. Photos by Doug Newman

sulted in some 1,000 old and rare photographs, many of which are on display in the museum today.

At the annual picnic in 1954 the group voted to affiliate with the Oregon Historical Society, and in 1955 the Lane County society was incorporated. Its stated objective was to "gather, preserve, and make available a museum, records, and other materials relating to the history of Lane County; to stimulate an interest in and knowledge of the locality's past, to carry on the tradition of the pioneer picnic, and to preserve and enlarge the museum collection."

Since that time the society has continuously pursued that goal. Working hand in hand with the Friends of the Museum, the organization co-hosts events of a historical nature, acts as a clearinghouse for information about the county's heritage, sponsors talks at schools, and handles specific requests—about genealogy or place names, for example—from the public.

The society was instrumental in the restoration of the 1853 county clerk's office, which is on display at the museum, and in the preservation and reassembly of the steam engine now in front of the museum. The organization also oversaw the building and placement of a replica of Eugene Skinner's log cabin, which was built in Oakridge in 1970 and which now stands in Skinner Butte Park.

The group's name was changed to the Lane County Historical Society in the mid-1960s to indicate that members need not be descendants of pioneers. Today the society, under the longtime leadership of outgoing president Hallie Huntington, has a membership of about 400 and is open to anyone interested in Lane County history.

CONE LUMBER COMPANY

In 1888 Joseph Cone, a Kansas farmer, packed up his family and headed west to join his two brothers at the sawmill they had established in 1886 in Clark County, Washington. In 1894 the Cone family moved to Troutdale, Oregon, where the three brothers—Joseph, George, and Harlan—built another mill. But Troutdale wasn't close enough to Portland to suit the brothers, so they sold that first Oregon mill and opened another in University Park. When that mill was sold, yet another was built at Lents. That one stayed in operation until 1909, when the brothers' partnership was dissolved, the mill sold, and Joseph moved to a farm in Laurel.

However, that was not the end of the Cone family's sawmill days in Oregon; indeed, it was just the beginning. After five years on the farm, Joseph was eager to return to the lumber business and opened a sawmill near Lone Rock, in Gilliam County. Earle Cone, the eldest of Joseph and Irissa Cone's six children, joined the business in Lone Rock briefly, but the family closed the mill in 1921.

Two years later Earle and his brothers, Ransom and Clarence, joined their father in buying a sawmill in Anlauf, a few miles from Cottage Grove. The mill did

well, cutting Douglas fir logs into railroad ties for the Southern Pacific Railroad, and the entire Cone family lived in Cottage Grove.

There were hardships ahead, however. In 1926 Joseph Cone died at the age of sixty-five, and two years later Irissa passed away. In 1929 the Depression forced the closing of the Anlauf mill. Assistance came in the form of the National Recovery Act, which artificially raised the price of lumber.

The Anlauf mill reopened in 1932 and operated until 1934, when Earle and Ransom traded it for a cedar mill in Oakridge. The two brothers ran the mill during the week and returned to their families in Cottage Grove on weekends—until the morning the mill burned down. After that, the brothers went their separate ways.

In business for himself, Earle suffered yet another mill fire, but persevered and bought a mill at Saginaw in 1935 which was operated for three years until it burned. Earle then managed to buy another facility at Goshen, site of the present Cone Lumber Company. The year was 1938, and the mill was one of only two in Oregon run by electricity. While his son, Edwin, finished university, Earle ran the plant alone, employing thirty men and cutting about

Edwin Cone (center, in dark jacket) and Earle Cone (sixth to the right of Edwin) with the Goshen mill crew members in May 1939.

40,000 board feet per day. In 1942 he suffered a heart attack, and Ed took over as general manager of the mill. Earle died in 1945 at the age of sixty-one, and his son has been running the mill ever since.

Under Ed Cone, who also served as mayor of Eugene from 1958 to 1969, Cone Lumber Company's original plant grew to include a new planing mill, dry kilns, log debarkers, chippers, and an additional sawmill. Ed and June Cone's three sons—Richard, Douglas, and Gregory—work in the business today, continuing a family tradition in Oregon that began almost 100 years ago.

The Lone Rock sawmill sometime between 1914 and 1921.

CHEF FRANCISCO

Chef Francisco, today a multimillion-dollar food production and processing corporation with headquarters in Eugene, began in 1946 when Fred Brunner started processing and freezing tamales, which he sold to grocery stores. His company, Chet's, was one of the first in the frozen food industry. Brunner soon added a broad line of frozen grocery products, including meat pies, fruit pies, and TV dinners, which he marketed to grocery outlets and later to distributors under the Chet's Famous Foods label.

Business boomed through the 1950s, but by the early 1960s larger frozen food corporations were underselling Chet's, and Brunner sold his operation to Mannings Fine Foods in 1963. Mannings, which included a cafeteria chain as well as a food service for institu-

tions such as hospitals and schools, used the Eugene frozen food plant as a central kitchen to process more than 300 products for its operations on the West Coast. Mannings eventually discontinued the original Chet's line of frozen foods—except for the tamales.

The Eugene plant manufactured, almost literally, everything from soup to cakes for Mannings until 1969, when it was sold to John Labatt Ltd., a Canadian corporation with interests in the food industry. Labatt had wanted to name its new acquisition Chef Eugene in honor of its location, but that name had already been used. Mannings' headquarters, however, had been located in San Francisco,

Fred Brunner oversees the production of tamales in the late 1940s.

and, as a result, Chef Francisco was born.

John Labatt Ltd. planned to use the Eugene plant to manufacture Mannings' products for sale to other restaurant operators. In 1971 Labatt expanded the Eugene plant and developed a broad line of convenience foods aimed at finer restaurants. By 1974, however, approximately two-thirds of Chef Francisco sales was still going to Mannings operations. The remaining third was going to other food service operators, primarily in the Northwest.

It was around that time that Chef Francisco began preparing foods for airlines as well. Development of a carrot cake that could be frozen, thawed, and would still taste moist and homemade was a breakthrough for the firm. Eastern Airlines, TWA, and other major

carriers bought the cake, and, for the first time, Chef Francisco was selling its products nationwide.

In 1975 the company decided to alter its original concept of marketing a broad range of frozen items in favor of concentrating on a few products marketed to major food-service operations. This strategy was a success, and shortly after Chef Francisco's carrot cake began appearing on airline meal trays, it was also being offered in Denny's and Sambo's national chains of restaurants.

Marketed under the Oregon Farms label created by Chef Francisco, the carrot cake also became a popular retail item. In 1980 Chef Francisco bought a bakery in King of Prussia, Pennsylvania, from Stouffer's, where it produces carrot cake, crumb cake, and cupcakes. With its products distributed nationwide, Oregon Farms has become the third-largest frozen cake brand in the country.

Meanwhile, Chef Francisco was also expanding in other areas. In the late 1970s soup had become a popular restaurant menu item, but soup of a consistently high quality is difficult for a restaurant to make. Chef Francisco marketed a frozen soup to which a cook need only add water or milk—and it always tasted good. Chef Francisco expanded the Eugene plant to include the largest frozen soup operation in the country. The soups are also processed in the Pennsylvania plant, and the firm now has the major share of the frozen soup market in the United States.

Chef Francisco has continued to expand in the 1980s. Today it includes an Arkansas company that processes sweet potato patties for restaurants, a Nebraska firm that is the country's largest processor of frozen breaded hors d'oeuvres, and an Ontario, Canada, manufacturer of frozen breaded products.

The firm's products are sold in thousands of restaurants throughout the United States and Canada. They appear on menus in hospital cafeterias and at colleges and universities. The Ontario plant is the world's largest processor of smelt, and Chef Francisco is marketing both smelt and carrot cake in Japan.

But Eugene is home. The local plant, which employs about 350 workers, accounts for more than 30 percent of the firm's multimillion-dollar sales. And Chef Francisco's corporate headquarters—somewhat posher, perhaps, than Fred Brunner's first office at the tamale factory—is still located in Eugene.

Fred Brunner's Chet's label, manufactured here, was sold to Mannings before becoming Chef Francisco under John Labatt Ltd.

THE REGISTER-GUARD

In 1867 John B. Alexander founded Eugene City's *Guard,* a Democratic weekly newspaper, but his tenure as publisher was short, and by the end of 1868 J.W. Skaggs was in charge of the paper. His tenure was even shorter; after five weeks Skaggs offered one of his printers, William Thompson, the handpress, the type, and two cords of wood to take the publication off his hands. Thompson agreed and became co-publisher with fellow printer William Victor.

These figures were only the beginning in a rapid succession of publishers and owners for the *Guard* from its founding to 1906. In 1877 Ira and John R. Campbell purchased the *Guard,* and it was under the Campbells that the paper became a daily in 1890. Ira Campbell was one of the founders of the Oregon Press Association. Charles H. Fisher bought out the Campbells in 1907, and five years later sold the paper to E.J. Finnerman, who installed a web-perfecting press that far exceeded the requirements of the paper's 5,000 circulation.

In 1916 Fisher returned to the *Guard* from the *Capital Journal* in Salem and, with J.E. Shelton, purchased the paper. After Fisher's death in 1924 the paper was sold to Paul R. Kelty, who in turn sold the *Guard* on March 1, 1927, to Alton F. Baker for just under $100,000.

The management of the Eugene Register-Guard *has been a Baker family operation, now into the third generation. Around 1956 father and sons posed for this photograph. Pictured are Alton F. Baker (seated) and his sons (standing, from left to right) Richard A. Baker, Edwin M. Baker, Alton F. Baker, Jr., and Herbert C. Baker.*

Baker came from a newspaper family. His father, Elbert H. Baker, was publisher of the Cleveland *Plain Dealer,* and his brother Frank was a newspaper publisher in Tacoma, Washington. Alton Baker came to Eugene from Cleveland expressly to buy the newspaper, and he soon brought to Eugene William Tugman, a reporter from the *Plain Dealer,* who became managing editor of the *Guard.*

Baker purchased the competing *Morning Register* in November 1930, and consolidated the two newspapers. The *Register* had been founded in 1899 by two brothers, Will G. and W. Frank Gilstrap, and had provided the city with a Republican viewpoint and staid editorial voice. Many of the *Register's* employees were taken on at the new *Eugene Register-Guard* after the consolidation. In October 1942 the *Eugene Register-Guard* purchased the circulation of the *Morning News,* which had begun publication in 1931, and Eugene became a one-newspaper town.

The management of the *Eugene Register-Guard* has been a Baker family operation, now into the third generation. In 1950 Alton F. Baker, Jr., was named managing editor and Tugman was advanced to the position of editor. Four years later Alton Jr. became editor and his brother, Edwin M. "Ted," who had moved through the ranks on the advertising and business side of the operation, was named business manager. Herbert C. Baker followed his brother as managing editor in 1955, and on March 1, 1961, Alton Jr. became editor and publisher, and Edwin Baker was named general manager.

At that time Alton Baker, Sr., assumed the position of chairman of the board of Guard Publishing Company. He served in that capac-

ity until his death in October of that year. Also in 1961 Richard A. Baker was appointed managing editor, a post he held until 1964, when he left to supervise another family publishing enterprise. He returned to the *Eugene Register-Guard* in 1977 as circulation director. In March 1982 Edwin Baker was named president and publisher, and Alton F. Baker, Jr., was named chairman of the board and editor.

Meanwhile, a third generation of Bakers joined the ranks at the *Eugene Register-Guard*. Tony Baker was named city editor in 1980 and two years later moved to the post of managing editor; Fletcher Little, son of Louise Baker Little, became advertising manager; and Bridget Baker, after working in the circulation department, became promotion manager.

Through the years the *Eugene Register-Guard* has grown in circulation and in stature, just as Eugene has grown in size and importance. In 1966 the paper won the bronze medal for "Distinguished Service to Journalism" awarded by the prestigious University of Missouri School of Journalism. It was the first time a small city daily outside of Missouri was so honored. The paper has repeatedly received the General Excellence Award presented by the Oregon Newspaper Publishers Association.

In addition, the *Eugene Register-Guard* has won many national awards, including the Penney-Missouri Award for Oregon Life and the Daily General Excellence

Award from the Associated Press Sports Editors for the sports department. In the 1970s, under graphics editor Brian Lanker, the *Eugene Register-Guard* became an innovator in the use of photographics and graphic images and developed a national reputation for its outstanding layout and design. In 1983 the paper dropped the word "Eugene" from its name to better emphasize its growing role as a regional newspaper, and that same year *The Register-Guard* changed from afternoon to morning publication to provide more timely sports, local, and market news for its 70,000 subscribers.

But growth has not been limited to circulation and reputation. The *Guard* has also expanded its physical plant to meet the needs of a growing readership over the years. In 1952, when circulation reached over 30,000, the paper moved from 1044 Willamette Street to 975 High Street, and a color convertible letterpress was installed in the

new building. A second floor was added to the building in 1966, and two more units of press were added in 1968, when circulation climbed above 50,000.

Updates of building and equipment continued with the purchase of a ten-unit offset press, and in 1979 the newsroom and other departments were completely remodeled. Today *The Register-Guard* has one of the most modern production facilities in the nation. The computer system is constantly being upgraded, and the newspaper is beginning the transition to electronically transmitted page layouts—called pagination.

After a shaky start with the revolving-door ownership of the original *Guard, The Register-Guard* has emerged as a growing example of professional journalism in the community. Indeed, it is today still meeting the demands of what its stated goal has been since the days of Alton Baker, Sr.: to be "a citizen of its community."

This early 1900s photograph shows the first office of the Guard. *Pictured are Pat Howe (second from left), who served the paper for over fifty years, and Charles Fisher (second from right), then editor and publisher.*

SACRED HEART GENERAL HOSPITAL

In 1936 the Sisters of St. Joseph of Newark, now known as the Sisters of St. Joseph of Peace, purchased Eugene's financially troubled Pacific Christian Hospital at the request of a group of local physicians. The Sisters who came to revive and revamp the facility brought it a new name and a new philosophy of health care. The name, Sacred Heart General Hospital, remains today; and the philosophy of the Sisters guides the

Pediatrics is just one of the areas that has grown in response to the physical, spiritual, and emotional necessities of the community, and to fulfill the Sisters' mission to reach those in need.

delivery of health care.

That philosophy emphasizes not only the healing of physical illness, but also extends a commitment to care for the emotional, spiritual, and social aspects of patients' lives. Sacred Heart, now a 422-bed facility with more than 1,800 employees, provides care to all in need regardless of economic status, just as the Sacred Heart of the 1930s did.

Indeed, growth in response to community needs has been an almost constant state at the hospital, beginning in the 1940s with physical expansion and the development of such specialized areas as pediatric care and rehabilitation. The Sisters' mission to reach those in need has been realized in later decades through various programs that go beyond care of the traditional hospital patient. In 1978 Sacred Heart began offering wellness and health classes to the public, and today a wide range of support groups and health and fitness classes attempt to educate and to promote healthful life-style changes.

Helping patients minimize hospital costs and life disruption has been a goal of the outpatient surgery unit, which opened in 1973. Its new home, which opened in 1979, was the first unit in Oregon developed specifically for outpatient surgery. The Short-Stay Unit continues to be a leader in delivering cost-effective, one-day surgery.

But new designs in inpatient care have not been forgotten, and the Cancer Care Center at Sacred Heart is perhaps the best example

of this. The Center represents the development of a coordinated program to deal with cancer patients—physically, spiritually, and emotionally. The Center features private rooms for patients as well as areas where patients can socialize and dine with their families in a relaxed atmosphere. Again, looking beyond physical needs, the Center stresses patient education and includes a hospice program to help the terminally ill and their families cope with the future.

It's a long way from the foundering Pacific Christian Hospital of 1936 to the modern institution of today, with its helipad for emergencies and its mobile cardiology van for testing patients in the community. But the underlying philosophy of the Sisters of St. Joseph of Peace hasn't changed—it's alive and well at Sacred Heart General Hospital.

The Sisters of St. Joseph of Newark, now the Sisters of St. Joseph of Peace, purchased the financially troubled Pacific Christian Hospital in 1936. With a new philosophy of health care came a new name, Sacred Heart General Hospital.

EUGENE MOVING AND STORAGE COMPANY

In March 1899 the stern-wheeler *City of Eugene* steamed its way down the Willamette River to Oregon City for the first time, offering merchants and residents of Eugene, Salem, and Portland the opportunity to literally ship freight from point to point rather than sending it by the more time-consuming and expensive overland route.

The steamboat, dubbed "The Freak" by irreverent Portlanders because it resembled Mississippi paddle wheelers of some forty

The Eugene Transfer Co., forerunner of Eugene Moving and Storage Company, existed (according to courthouse records) as early as 1880. At the time of this photo, around 1912, it was owned by W.L. Christensen, who ran the business for thirty-five years.

Today Eugene Moving and Storage Company, in marked contrast to its horse-drawn wagons of earlier years, has three long-haul vans, three local vans, and two service vehicles to handle an average 1,000 moves a year.

years earlier, was sponsored by the Eugene Transfer Co. and was operated by the firm in partnership with the City of Eugene. It carried furniture and other goods, along with passengers, between Eugene and Portland until 1905.

For generations it was thought that the formation of the organization to sponsor and operate the *City of Eugene* marked the birth of the Eugene Transfer Co., which later became Eugene Moving and Storage Company. However, docu-

ments found at the courthouse in the 1950s showed that the Eugene Transfer Co. existed as early as 1880, when E.J. McClanahan did street and alley cleaning for the city under that name.

McClanahan, who had come to Eugene in 1866, owned the first pair of trucks (horse-drawn) in Eugene, and for years was the only local drayman. He is, however, not mentioned as among those involved in the riverboat experiment early in this century.

In 1906 the Eugene Transfer Co. was owned by E.M. Cooper and W.J. Williams and was located at 559 1/2 Willamette. W.L. Christensen became the owner in 1912 and ran the business for thirty-five years. When Walter Holleque bought the firm in 1946, it consisted of two prewar vans and a small leased warehouse and office at 40 West Seventh Avenue. Holleque asked his brother-in-law, Gus Hixson, to join him in the enterprise, and the company became the family operation that it remains today.

That same year Eugene Transfer became the local agent for Lyon Van Lines, but switched in 1947 to North American Van Lines since Lyon did not serve the East Coast. In the years since, Eugene Trans-

fer has won numerous awards for outstanding service as a North American agency.

The firm moved to its present site, at 260 Ferry Street, in 1950, and since then everything from grand pianos to food-filled deep freezers have been stored in its 20,000-square-foot, temperature-controlled concrete warehouse. In 1957 Hixson's son, Robert, joined the company, which was incorporated as Eugene Moving and Storage in 1961. Harvey Lounsbury, Jr., also Holleque's brother-in-law, joined the firm in 1963, and today is president and co-owner, with Robert Hixson as vice-president. Continuing the family nature of the business, Lounsbury's daughter, Gail, joined the firm in 1980.

Eugene Moving and Storage Company, which began with a horse-drawn wagon, now has three long-haul vans, three local vans, and two service vehicles. In 1984 it handled about 1,000 moves—and it didn't need a steamboat for a single one.

McKAY INVESTMENT COMPANY

Miles E. McKay, founder of McKay Investment Company and former partner in McKay's Markets, is a native Oregonian—just barely. He was born in the town of Ontario in 1912 while his family was traveling west from Michigan. After his birth they moved on and settled in Eugene, where he later attended Eugene High School and the University of Oregon. During his school years the young McKay worked at Safeway and at Everett Eggelston's Economy Grocery, developing an interest in the grocery business.

McKay bought his first grocery store, at 675 River Road, in 1939. However, World War II interrupted his budding career. He sold the store in 1942 when he joined the Army and moved with his wife, Eleanor, and their two small children to Seattle, where he was stationed. The family returned to Eugene after the war, and in 1946 McKay bought a little grocery store at Marcola. His brother, Kenny, bought a grocery store on River Road at about the same time, and shortly thereafter Miles and Harold Hagg, a family friend, bought another store at Veneta.

The McKay's Markets chain was born when the two McKays and Hagg formed a partnership and brought all three stores under the same name. A fourth store was built on River Road, and Dean McKay, another brother, joined the partnership. The operation proved to be a great success, and by 1959 McKay's Markets included sixteen stores in the Eugene metropolitan area, Salem, and Roseburg. That year all the stores were sold to Mayfair Markets, and Miles McKay began devoting all of his energies to McKay Investment Company, an enterprise he had started in 1953.

The firm was begun as a part-

Miles McKay, founder of McKay Investment Company and former partner in McKay's Markets.

nership consisting of Miles, Eleanor, and their two children, Linda and Doug. The company that was later to develop the Oakway Mall began with the purchase of a rental property at the corner of Seventh and Pearl that consisted of Billy's grocery store and two apartments. But McKay Investment grew quickly, and in 1956 the firm bought land on Coburg Road and embarked on its first major construction job—a commercial building that originally housed a McKay's Market and a Tiffany's drugstore and today houses a Mark N Pak store.

The Coburg Road development was a meaningful project for the McKay family and for McKay Investments. It established a pattern, still followed by the firm today, of developing properties rather than buying buildings. In 1962 the com-

pany was the first to build commercially in the Mohawk area of Springfield and also gained control of property that was to be the site of McKay Investment's largest project—the Oakway Mall. Construction began on the mall in 1966, and Tiffany's and Albertson's opened stores there later that year. Each year one building was added to the property until 1979, when it was fully developed.

The mall itself is a fitting monument for a family-owned and -operated business now in its third generation. The land had been the site of the old Hayes farm, where Miles McKay's father had lived with his second wife, Lillie Hayes,

Miles McKay bought his first grocery store at 675 River Road in 1939. The building is still in use as the River Road Hardware Store.

after his first wife died. The mall was developed to leave landmarks to the farm, with a large fir tree left to mark the site of the farmhouse and a grassy area with five remaining oak trees to mark where the barn had been.

Today J. Douglas McKay and Linda McKay Korth are more active than their parents in the management of McKay Investment Company. And their children, Tracie and Amy McKay and Kelly, Kim, and Steve Korth, are beginning to take their places within the firm, ensuring the continuation of a familiar family business name with strong roots in the community.

Located on River Road, this was the first grocery store built by McKay's Markets in 1950.

LANE COMMUNITY COLLEGE

The main campus of Lane Community College, at 4000 East Thirtieth Avenue, opened in 1968.

When Lane Community College opened its doors in 1965, it opened a lot of them: in garages, storefronts, abandoned laundries, elementary school buildings, wherever space was available for a fledgling college to hold a class. That first year the college offered thirteen state-approved vocational programs as well as college transfer courses and adult education classes. Some 1,500 students enrolled and shared in the frustrations and the excitement of being a part of a bold new educational endeavor.

Developing a community college was more complicated than finding a storefront and signing up students; it had to start with an idea. The idea for a community college that would serve all of Lane County and then some, encompassing twenty-three school districts and 5,000 square miles, took shape in 1964. At that time administrators from eight school districts and Senator Glen Stadler formed the Community College Study Committee to assess the popularity of the idea and to generate enthusiasm for the concept in the community.

What was to become Lane Community College actually had its beginnings in 1938 with the establishment of Eugene Vocational School, which became Eugene Technical-Vocational School twenty years later. The proposed community college would, according to the vision of its proponents, absorb that school and go far beyond its limited scope.

The idea sparked interest among citizens' groups, and petitions were circulated for a referendum, which was held on October 19, 1964. Voter turnout was slim, but the results were overwhelming. The referendum passed by a five-to-one majority, giving Oregon its ninth community college district. In 1965 a $9.9-million bond issue and a $2-million serial levy were approved, materially paving the way for the development of the college's present campus in the Russell Creek Basin at Interstate 5 and Thirtieth Avenue, which opened in September 1968.

The true focus of the new college was clear in the make-up of the seven-member board that was elected when the initial referendum was passed. Of twenty-three candidates, all those elected had supported the concept of a "comprehensive" college, not just another junior college or a vocational training center. From the beginning the emphasis at LCC has been on innovation and service to the whole community.

That tradition was begun by the first board and nurtured by the college's first president, Dale Parnell. In 1968 Parnell was recruited for the state superintendent's job, but the tradition was carried on by acting president Robert Hamill in 1968, by president Robert Pickering in 1969, and by Eldon G. Schafer, president from 1970 to 1985. The current president is Richard M. Turner III.

Over the years the number of vocational programs has increased to fifty, and in 1972 the school was named one of the six best comprehensive, technical-vocational community colleges in the country. The following year LCC was invited to join the League for Innovation in the Community College, a national organization of seventeen leading community college districts.

But creating an outstanding selection of vocational programs has been only part of the innovation process. For example, the concept of adult education has grown and changed with the needs of the community. In the early 1970s business courses were among the most popular adult classes. They were low-cost, noncredit courses usually offered at night. In 1976, faced with an increasing demand for business-oriented courses, LCC started a three-year Farm Management program. The following year it instituted a three-year Small

Fountains and beautiful landscaping highlight Lane Community College's main campus.

Business Management program, which was later recognized by the Oregon Department of Education as the state's best post-secondary vocational program.

Through such programs, the college has taken education to the community, sharing faculty expertise with those beyond the schoolroom doors. The concept of adult education evolved into community education, and in 1982 LCC's

Business Assistance Center opened its doors. In its first two years the center assisted more than 3,000 businesses and 5,000 individuals.

The individual has continued to be of prime importance to LCC—the individual student, the individual teacher, and the individual resident of the district. During the late 1960s many of the students were veterans; many others were adults who had dropped out of previous schools and were looking for a nonintimidating reentry into the educational process. In the 1970s women began returning to school after having spent years at home rearing children. LCC responded by developing a strong student support system, featuring individual counseling interviews and a variety of educational and career counseling services available to all district residents.

In 1977 the college was cited by the American Association of Community and Junior Colleges for having exemplary outreach, counseling, and vocational testing programs for women. Students benefit, too, from the caring attitude of a faculty chosen, in the words of one administrator, because they are "good human beings and really committed to teaching."

Today Lane Community College has an enrollment of approximately 31,000, and has adjunct facilities at the Siuslaw Area Center, built in 1976 in Florence; at the Downtown Center, which opened in 1977 at 1059 Willamette in Eugene; and at the Central Area Education Center, which began operation in 1981 in Cottage Grove. In addition, a fully equipped mobile classroom began serving outlying areas of the district in 1977. The University of Texas at Austin did a national study of the leading community colleges and Lane Community College ranked number three.

LOCHMEAD FARMS/DARI-MART STORES

It just didn't make sense for the head of the Agriculture Education Department at Oregon Agricultural College (now Oregon State University), not to own a bit of farmland. So in 1941 Heber Gibson and his wife, Edith, along with their son, Howard, and his wife, Gladys, bought 160 acres 4.5 miles north of Junction City. The elder Gibsons did not live on the farm, but their son, a former vocational agriculture instructor, and his wife settled right in, raising sheep, turkeys, and vegetable seed crops.

Howard Gibson, with a bow to his Scottish heritage, would later call the place Lochmead Farms, a name that eventually would become emblazoned on refrigerator trucks and milk containers and would be familiar throughout the area as a major independent milk processor and distributor.

The business really got its start in the late 1940s, when Gibson built a milking parlor and the first dairy buildings on the farm. That first parlor took 100 cows, which the Gibsons had bought as calves from Tillamook for ten dollars a head. The family sold milk to processors and distributors while slowly expanding the operation and adding land.

In 1964 the younger Gibsons and their three sons, Jock, Warren, and Mike, formed a corporation and decided to process their own milk and retail it through their own outlet. The next year, with 350 cows, they began building the processing plant in Junction City. The front of the plant housed the first Dari-Mart, a drive-up dairy store that also carried a few grocery items. Another Dari-Mart in Springfield, one in Corvallis, and two in Eugene rounded out the retail operation.

The sixth store, built in Eugene in the late 1960s, began the transition for Dari-Mart from dairy stores to walk-in convenience markets. Since then the chain has built an average of one store per year, all within a forty-mile radius of Junction City. Over the years the corporation has acquired more land and expanded the dairy operation as well.

In 1970 the Gibsons built an entirely new dairy complex with state-of-the-art equipment to handle their 500 cows. The farm itself, where feed for the cows is still grown, expanded to include parts of six adjacent farms and today encompasses some 1,000 acres. Sons Warren and Mike and their families live on the farm, where crops include peppermint as well as bush beans, sweet corn, and peas, which are sold for processing and freezing. In 1981 the corporation bought a peppermint distillery in Harrisburg and entered the custom peppermint-harvesting business.

But the dairy is still the focal point of the business—and of the family. And at Lochmead Farms/ Dari-Mart Stores, it is tough to separate the two. Howard Gibson is president of Lochmead Farms and Gladys is president of the 25-store Dari-Mart operation. Jock is in charge of the processing operation, and Warren is the dairyman. Their wives, Mary Jane and Elizabeth, handle marketing and promotion for Dari-Mart. Mike runs the farm, with the help of his wife, Tani. A Gibson daughter, Pat

In 1970 the Gibsons built an entirely new dairy complex with state-of-the-art equipment to handle their 500 cows.

One of the twenty-five Dari-Mart stores, all built within a forty-mile radius of Junction City.

Straube, is office manager of the corporation, and her husband, Gary, became general manager of the Dari-Mart stores in 1974. Indeed, the Lochmead Farms/ Dari-Mart Stores corporation is basically just an Oregon family farm—with a milking parlor that produces 3,500 gallons a day and a still-growing chain of stores in which to sell it.

CLARKE'S SHEET METAL, INC.

Clarke's Sheet Metal, Inc., began in 1952 as a family-owned shop at 368 High Street in Eugene. In those very early days Ralph Clarke had two helpers: his wife, Belle, and their son, Jim, who had just returned from Korea with the First Marine Division.

Today Clarke's is still a family-owned operation, but the family spans three generations, and the operation employs well over 100 sheet-metal workers, engineers, sales representatives, and office personnel. The corporation that began as a two-man shop on High Street has evolved into a major designer of innovative wood-processing equipment, and recently was named Business Exporter of the Month in honor of its commercial exports to Africa, Asia, Europe, and South America by the Willamette Valley World Trade Committee.

The corporation's president and co-founder, Ralph H. Clarke, got his start in the sheet-metal industry in 1926 when he worked for the Chase Co. in Eugene. His first major job was sheet-metal work on McArthur Court on the University of Oregon campus. He stayed with Chase until 1937, when he opened the Valley Metal Co., at Seventh and Oak, which he operated until 1941.

Clarke moved to Seattle and during the 1940s worked in sheet-metal shops in Seattle and Eugene. In 1951 he returned to Eugene for good, and the next year, with his wife and their son, opened the business that would ultimately be global in range.

Clarke's Sheet Metal grew almost from the start, and by only the second year of operation was a

six-man shop. As Eugene grew, so did the firm, doing sheet-metal work on the U.S. National Bank building at Eighth and Willamette, the Hilton Hotel, the Hult Center, major retail buildings at Valley River Center, and many dormitory and classroom buildings at the University of Oregon. In 1967

This replica of Clarke's first facility at Third and High streets was built by Bob Marshall, the firm's first employee, who retired after twenty years of service.

Clarke's built and moved into its present headquarters at 660 Conger Street.

Clarke attributes much of the corporation's steady growth over the years to its research and devel-

Clarke's Sheet Metal built and moved into its present headquarters, at 660 Conger Street, in 1967.

opment of new machinery, including innovative techniques and designs, and to the worldwide need for state-of-the-art mill equipment. Clarke's is now recognized as one of the top engineering manufacturers and installers of low- and high-pressure pneumatic systems. It continues to provide the woodworking industry with "total engineering" that results in everything from storage bins that stand ninety-four feet high, to spark detectors for industrial fire and explosion protection.

Today Ralph Clarke is president of Clarke's Sheet Metal, Inc.; W. James Clarke is vice-president; and Belle Clarke is secretary/treasurer. The corporation, along with Clarke's International, Inc., is a subsidiary of Clarke's Industries, Inc.—all operating out of Eugene. Clarke's Industries is also the parent corporation of Clarke's Southern in Atlanta, Georgia, and Allied Sheet Metal & Blow Pipe, Inc., in Shreveport, Louisiana.

THE WOODARD FAMILY FOUNDATION

At the age of ten, Walter A. Woodard traveled with his family to Oregon from their native Iowa. In 1900 the Woodard family settled in Cottage Grove, where young Walter was to become one of the area's lumber pioneers. He founded the W.A. Woodard Lumber Co. in the early 1920s, with the main part of the sawmill at the present Weyerhaeuser site on U.S. 99. The success of the mill was the stimulus for The W.A. Woodard Foundation, which was established by Walter Woodard in 1952 as a philanthropic organization.

The foundation, now known as The Woodard Family Foundation, was begun by Walter because, as his son Carlton says, "he liked to do charitable work particularly for Cottage Grove." And charitable work is what the foundation is all about.

Even before the foundation was established, Woodard was contributing generously to community causes. As chairman of the first Cottage Grove Hospital board, he was instrumental in the development and financing of that institution, which opened its doors in 1947. Two years later he constructed and donated to the city the Cottage Grove Public Library, which was completed in 1950. In 1972 the building, at Sixth and Washington, was rededicated and named the W.A. Woodard Memorial Library.

In 1951 Carlton Woodard founded Kimwood Corporation, a manufacturer of woodworking machinery, locating the operation just across U.S. 99 from the sawmill. When the foundation was established the next year, it became the charitable arm of the two companies. The lumber operation was sold to Weyerhaeuser Corporation in 1957, but the foundation was continued and was supported by

Walter A. Woodard, founder of what is now The Woodard Family Foundation.

later family enterprises, such as The Village Green Motor Hotel and The Valley River Inn, as well as by Kimwood.

Over the years the Woodard enterprises that support the organization have changed somewhat, but the foundation's aim has remained the same: to return something to the community. In recent years The Woodard Family Foundation has provided college scholarships for Cottage Grove High School students and has supported the Oregon Trail Council of the Boy Scouts of America, the Cottage Grove Hospital, University of Oregon, Lewis and Clark College, Junior Achievement, and a host of other area organizations.

The foundation's board has taken a great interest in education, providing scholarships at Lane Community College, the University of Oregon, Oregon State University, and other institutions. The family tradition of university support was evident as long ago as 1956, when Walter Woodard and his wife, Dutee, donated $5,640 to the University of Oregon Library for purchase of a rare fifteenth-century French manuscript.

As the name implies, the foundation is a family affair. Since the death of Walter Woodard in 1971, the board of directors of The Woodard Family Foundation has consisted of his wife, Dutee, who is vice-president; their son, Carlton, president; Carlton's wife, Joy; and two of their children, Kim and Kristen.

NIKE

When Bill Bowerman got out of the Army in 1946, he returned to his alma mater, the University of Oregon, where he had been a business major and an athlete. Bowerman's first love was track—he had coached high school track before the war—so he took a job as freshman football coach at the University of Oregon because it included the position of track coach.

But Bowerman could not find the kangaroo leather track shoes that had been available before the war and thought the cowhide shoes being made then were heavy and cumbersome. He decided to design a shoe for his runners himself, little realizing that this decision would eventually lead to development of a multimillion-dollar corporation with a name that would become synonymous with running to sports-minded people around the world—Nike.

A shoemaker on campus gave Bowerman a pair of size 10 lasts to get started with, and a maker of logging boots in Springfield cut out a rough shoe pattern on newspaper. Bowerman then began to make prototypes, using synthetic furniture covering material for the uppers because of its strength.

He tried out his first pair of shoes on Phillip Knight, a miler and half-miler on the university's track team. Otis Davis, who was later to be an Olympic gold medal winner, also streaked around the track in Bowerman's experimental shoes.

Not until the late 1950s, however, did Bowerman have a shoe he thought was suitable for competition. By that time his prototype was comfortable and light, made of kid leather rather than the usual cowhide, and weighing five ounces less than the common American track shoe. The weight difference translated into more energy for the runner during a race, so Bowerman began making a couple of dozen shoes per season for his runners.

Meanwhile, Phillip Knight, who had worn the first prototype, had graduated from the University of Oregon and had gone on to Stanford University to do graduate work in business; his thesis was on the marketing of shoes. He returned from a trip to Japan and suggested to Bowerman that they import and sell shoes from the Tiger Shoe Company in Kobi.

The two formed Blue Ribbon Sports and went into the shoe business. Knight's sister and Bowerman's son were the first salespeople, operating out of Knight's father's basement or the back of Bowerman's car at track meets. So Bowerman, in the early 1960s, was selling shoes, but not the shoes he had designed.

That changed in 1964 when he redesigned the Tiger shoe, making it flat and creating, essentially, the first shoe for joggers. About that same time he began experimenting with nylon as an ideal material for running and jogging shoes. In 1970 Bowerman, Knight, and a group of mostly local people set up a limited corporation, SportsTech, although the shoes were still being manufactured by Tiger in Japan.

In 1972 shoe sales reached two million dollars per year, and the corporation, to avoid problems with Tiger, established other manufacturing outlets in Japan and on the East Coast in the United States. It was also in 1972 that a new name for the corporation was adopted—Nike, after the Greek goddess of victory. Today Phillip Knight is president and Bill Bowerman is senior vice-president of the sports marketing empire that got its start because Knight needed shoes to run in and Bowerman decided to make them.

Bill Bowerman, track coach at the University of Oregon, hand-finishing a shoe he is designing for Nike production.

UNIVERSITY OF OREGON

On October 16, 1876, the State University of Oregon opened its doors, and 177 students and five faculty members walked through them and into history. The institution, chartered in 1872 and located in Eugene, at the time of its opening consisted of one building, Deady Hall. As one of those first students wrote: "It stood there in the stubble field from which the grain had recently been reaped. There were no trees save the noble oaks on the northeast corner."

Villard Hall was opened in 1886, doubling the classroom space, but the university was even then struggling through hard times. The faculty had taken a 25-percent salary reduction, and in 1881 railroad magnate Henry Villard saved the school from closure by paying $7,000 of its indebtedness. Financial problems were exacerbated by a perception that the education offered at the new university was not liberal enough, and in 1885 only four students graduated from the school, down from sixteen in 1883.

In its first years the university offered two courses of study toward a degree: the classical and the scientific. Each required six years and stressed the classical curriculum of the eastern schools in the Victorian period and included classes in Latin, Greek, and Astronomy. This changed somewhat under the administration of Charles Hiram Chapman, who succeeded John Wesley Johnson, the school's first president, in 1893. Chapman liberalized the curriculum and introduced the idea of elective courses.

Those first students lived wherever they might find room in the small town of Eugene, but in 1893 Friendly Hall, the first dormitory, was built. The north entrance to the building was for women, the south for men, and the living areas

Villard Hall, opened in 1886, has national landmark status.

were divided by a wall. Despite such precautions, the coed living arrangement was frowned upon, and the following year Friendly Hall became an all-male dormitory.

By the turn of the century the University of Oregon boasted a half-dozen buildings and 456 students—students who were beginning to feel the independent spirit of the new era. In 1900 the Associated Students organization was founded, and the *Oregon Weekly,* which was to become the *Oregon Daily Emerald* by 1920, began publication.

The university grew phenomenally in the early 1900s, and by 1919 there were 1,839 students, almost twice the enrollment of 1915. Under president Prince Lucien Campbell, the School of Architecture and the School of Commerce were created in 1914, the Law Department was made a school in 1915, the School of Journalism was established in 1916, and the School of Health and Physical Education, the first in the nation, was created in 1920. Ellis Lawrence, who came to the campus in 1915 as dean of the new Architecture School, per-

haps more than any other figure left his mark on the physical aspect of the campus; he designed every building erected there from 1915 to 1944, a total of nineteen structures.

But close on the heels of those early boom years came the 1930s, rough times for the university, as they were for most of the state, the nation, and the world. The Depression caused a decline in enrollment, from 3,500 in 1929 to 2,400 four years later, and many students who were enrolled needed

An early view of the University of Oregon campus.

jobs to survive and loans to pay tuition fees. In 1931 the Zorn-Mac-Pherson Bill, which would have abolished the university by merging it with Oregon State College in Corvallis, was overwhelmingly defeated at the polls.

The year 1935 saw a huge peace march on campus, and the faculty agreed to dismiss classes for one hour in support of peace. But peace marches notwithstanding, when war was declared in 1941

Sports have always played a role in campus life at the University of Oregon. Pictured is the school's 1899 football team.

University of Oregon students went to fight. The overcrowding that resulted when the GIs returned to campus in 1946 was unprecedented, and temporary housing sprang up in the form of trailer houses and Quonset huts for married students.

The 1960s and 1970s were tumultuous years for the university, with student political activities and unrest mirroring what was happening across the country. The excitement of sorority and fraternity rush, of "Sweethearts" and "Homecoming" that had dominated the 1950s was gone, and campus activities took the form of rallies and demonstrations.

Arthur Flemming was president for most of the 1960s, and, despite the growing unrest, he saw univer-

sity enrollment increase as well as an expansion in both faculty and curriculum. In 1966 the School of Librarianship was established, the first professional school to be added since 1920.

Flemming was followed by Robert D. Clark, who was university president from 1969 to 1975, perhaps the school's most troubling years, with student unrest over racial issues and the war in Vietnam. The Honors College, which he had founded in 1950, was named for Clark upon his retirement.

Campus political activities de-

clined as the war wound down, and the university in the first half of the 1980s has emerged as one of the outstanding public institutions of higher learning in the country. The University of Oregon is one of only twenty-four public institutions selected for membership in the distinguished Association of American Universities. Its individual schools have attained national reputations for excellence in instruction and in research.

Today the university is composed of a comprehensive College of Arts and Sciences and professional schools in architecture and allied arts, business administration, education, human development and performance, journalism, law, and music. Research facilities include the internationally recognized Institute of Molecular Biology, the Solar Energy Center, and the new Institute of Neuroscience and the Chemical Physics Institute.

What was once a building in a field of stubble is today a campus of 250 acres, itself an arboretum for the study of more than 400 varieties of trees. There are eighty-two buildings, two of which—Deady and Villard halls—have national landmark status. Through financial difficulties, an attempt to abolish the school itself, student unrest, and two world wars, the spirit that marked the first students and faculty of the University of Oregon has not flagged, and the devotion of the institution's supporters has not waned. For more than 100 years the University of Oregon has continued to grow, increasing its enrollment and its stature both in the community and throughout the nation.

Today the University of Oregon's eighty-two buildings rest on 250 acres. Pictured is Fenton Hall. © 1982, University of Oregon

137

POOLE-LARSEN FUNERAL HOME AND CREMATORIUM

Arthur W. Larsen served his embalming and funeral directing apprenticeship under Charles Poole. In 1944 he purchased the Poole Funeral Home, renaming it Poole-Larsen Funeral Home.

In 1960 Theodore A. Larsen joined his father's firm.

In 1927 Charles Poole opened the Poole Funeral Home at 1100 Charnelton Street. Today that building houses the Poole-Larsen Funeral Home.

In 1927 Charles Poole, a licensed funeral director and embalmer who owned a funeral home in Springfield, opened the Poole Funeral Home at 1100 Charnelton in Eugene. The building, which today houses the Poole-Larsen Funeral Home and Crematorium, had originally been a private residence and was later used as a convent by St. Mary's Catholic Church, which was located across the street. Poole completely remodeled the building, and that first year the Poole Funeral Home served about twenty-five families in the community.

Business grew steadily, and in 1931 Arthur W. Larsen served his embalming and funeral directing apprenticeship under Poole. Larsen, who had graduated from the University of Oregon in 1929, was licensed as an embalmer and funeral director in 1933 and worked for funeral homes in Klamath Falls and Medford for the next eleven years. He returned to Eugene in 1944 and bought the Poole Funeral Home, renaming it Poole-Larsen Funeral Home.

Before selling his operation to Larsen, Poole had been a major in-novator in funeral home services in the area by installing a crematorium on the premises. It was the only crematorium in Lane County until the mid-1950s and was routinely used by other funeral homes in the area that could not provide the service on their own.

Larsen continued that innovative spirit in 1944 when he began providing those attending funeral services with memorial folders that included the name of the deceased, biographical information, and a quotation from the Scriptures. Providing such remembrances is a common practice today among funeral homes, but, like cremation, it was pioneered in this area by Poole-Larsen.

In 1960 Theodore A. (Ted) Larsen joined his father's business and was licensed as a funeral director and embalmer the following year. Ted Larsen had grown up with the funeral business, living in or next door to funeral homes most of his life. He had graduated from the University of Oregon in 1957 and entered the Air Force as a second lieutenant. It was perhaps only natural that after his tour of duty in Korea and subsequent discharge, he turned to the family business. He became a partner with his father in 1968 and purchased his father's interest in the firm when Arthur Larsen retired in 1975. He died in April 1985 at the age of seventy-eight.

By 1968 extensive remodeling at the funeral home reflected a growing business. Additions included a chapel, family room, general public areas, and viewing rooms. There have been minor renovations since then, and in 1973 a new crematorium was installed.

Today Poole-Larsen Funeral Home and Crematorium coordinates services and burial and provides grief therapy and counseling for about 300 families each year. For twenty-six years the firm has been a member of the International Order of the Golden Rule, an organization of funeral homes whose members are invited to join based on recommendations by clergy, doctors, and other community leaders. It is an appropriate honor for the only funeral home in Lane County owned by the same family for more than forty years, and one that has served over 14,000 families in the community.

FIRST INTERSTATE BANK OF OREGON, N.A.

First Interstate Bank of Oregon, the oldest nationally chartered bank west of the Rocky Mountains, has been serving the greater Eugene-Springfield area for more than a century.

Early Lane County pioneers managed without banks. Then, in 1883, two prominent Eugene businessmen, T.G. Hendricks and S.B. Eakin, established a bank in Eugene as a private commercial enterprise. Although they had been preceded by a rival institution, the rival did not survive. Hendricks and Eakin, however, did survive and prosper, locating their bank on the west side of Willamette Street between Eighth Street and Broadway.

Hendricks and Eakin changed their bank to a federally chartered institution in 1886, and the name became First National Bank of Eugene. In 1898 the old Bristow-Hendricks general store, at the northwest corner of Willamette and Broadway, was remodeled to provide a new home for the bank. Eakin and Hendricks continued as the institution's chief officers until their deaths in 1912 and 1917, respectively.

Succeeding Hendricks as president were P.E. Snodgrass in 1917, A.A. Rogers in 1929, Richard Shore Smith in 1931, and Lynn S. McCready in 1945. McCready continued as president until February 8, 1954, when the institution was merged with the First National Bank of Portland, which would later be renamed First National Bank of Oregon. McCready was then named vice-president and manager of the Eugene branch. Prior to the merger, two additional branches of the original bank were established: the West Eugene Branch in August 1949 and the Springfield Branch in 1950.

On June 1, 1981, First National

First Interstate Bank of Oregon, the oldest nationally chartered bank west of the Rockies, was federally chartered in 1886 as First National Bank of Eugene. Courtesy, Lane County Museum

Bank of Oregon, successor to the First National Bank of Eugene, went through yet another name change when it became First Interstate Bank of Oregon, N.A. As such, it is an integral part of the First Interstate Bank system, serving thirteen Western states including Alaska and Hawaii. The bank recently added affiliates in two Midwestern states, Wisconsin and Iowa (effective in the summer of 1985).

There are more than 1,000 of-

fices and more than 900 Day and Night Teller machines to serve First Interstate Bank customers throughout the West. First Interstate is also a member of the CIRRUS network of automatic teller machines, giving customers access to cash at more than 6,600 locations throughout the United States and Canada.

The First Interstate Bank system is backed by over $45 billion in assets and is one of the largest retail banking systems in the country. Today there are more than 165 locations in Oregon, with 14 First Interstate branches serving the financial needs of residents and businesses in the Eugene-Springfield area.

DOW CORNING CORPORATION

What is now Dow Corning's silicon-manufacturing plant in Springfield, with its eighteen-megawatt furnace and approximately eighty employees, had its modest beginning as the National Metallurgical Corporation in January 1954. Jointly owned by Apex Smelting and American Smelting and Refining Companies, the 2.5-megawatt furnace was manned by twenty employees. Essentially a pilot plant, the small facility was erected to develop a commercial process for producing aluminum directly from low-grade ore. The resulting product was to be an alloy of aluminum and silicon, the latter being a metallic-like material added to aluminum to give it strength. Although technically feasible, the process was not economically viable, and the facility was converted to produce high-purity silicon metal, which it continues to do to this day.

The Pacific Northwest was an ideal area to locate a silicon-smelting operation in the 1950s. The market provided by all the major aluminum producers was nearby, and there was an abundance of low-cost hydroelectric power available, an important consideration for an energy-intensive industry. Indeed, the opening of the smelting plant was a major boost to the newly formed Springfield Utility Board and continues to provide the steady load base upon which the utility builds its system reliability and economical operation.

From that beginning the plant has continued to be very much a part of the local community, providing jobs for Springfield residents, purchasing supplies from local vendors, and supporting various community activities through the chamber of commerce and service clubs, and supporting various social, educational, and youth or-

Dow Corning is the world's largest producer of silicon-bearing materials. A worker is shown casting the 3,000-degree-Fahrenheit silicon.

ganizations.

Through the 1960s and early 1970s the operation continued to grow, with the modification of the original furnace and the addition of a second furnace. A change in ownership in late 1967 saw Kawecki-Berylco Industries acquire the facility, and the site was fitted with state-of-the-art fume collection to control air pollution in 1970. A large commercial furnace with newer and more efficient pollution-control equipment was installed in 1975 and is still in operation today. The old, smaller furnaces were retired.

Through the years the production of silicon at the Springfield plant was directed solely to the use in manufacturing special aluminum alloys. The acquisition of the facility in 1980 by Dow Corning Corporation provided much more than a name change. Dow Corning is the world's largest producer of silicon-bearing materials, manufacturing more than 2,000 products for such diverse industries as construction, petroleum and chemicals, food processing, electronics, automotive, paints, paper, personal

The operating floor of Dow Corning's silicon furnace building.

care, rubber, and many more. The plant currently produces solely for Dow Corning products.

Plant manager Frank A. Kosciolek is especially proud of the outstanding safety record Dow Corning has maintained throughout the years, and Kosciolek has been there for most of those years. Today, at the little plant that started on the outskirts of Springfield, he leads a managerial staff of five, supervising seventy-five additional employees in the production of 10,000 tons of silicon per year for one of the world's major industrial concerns.

WILLAMETTE POULTRY CO.

The Willamette Poultry Co., whose products are known to consumers under the Fircrest Foods label, was founded in 1959 when Edward Heyerly, along with Murray Collins, Ray Holt, and Richard Peterson, bought Miller's Poultry in Creswell. Heyerly was president of the new venture, which began operating with sixteen employees and a processing rate of 5,000 chickens per week. When Heyerly died in December 1984 Willamette Poultry employed 300 full-time workers, processed 150,000 chickens per week, and was on the verge of entering the international export market.

Indeed, in the years since 1959 the firm has looked to diversification, innovation, and expansion to turn a small chicken-processing plant into one of Oregon's 100-largest privately held companies. In addition to the Creswell offices and processing plant, Willamette Poultry now has warehouses in Bend and Medford and sales distribution plants in those two cities and in Clackamas County and Corvallis. Those 150,000 chickens per week come from farms owned by Fircrest Farms, a wholly owned subsidiary of Willamette Poultry, and from contract growers.

Ray Hooley, Heyerly's son-in-law, joined the business in 1960. Hooley became president of Willamette Poultry when Heyerly retired in 1967, and in 1978 he bought out the last of the original partners who had purchased Miller's Poultry.

In recent years there has been more to Willamette Poultry than chickens, although poultry is still the primary product. The Fircrest label has come to include french fries, hash browns, corn dogs, burritos, and wieners. In addition, in 1970 the firm began distributing a wide range of institutional foods,

In 1984 Willamette Poultry opened a $1.5-million addition to its Creswell plant, almost doubling its size.

including fish, vegetables, fruit, cakes, and pies. Some five years later the company expanded into private labeling of nonmeat items, and today 25 percent of the products it distributes are processed elsewhere.

In 1984 Willamette Poultry opened a $1.5-million addition to its Creswell plant that almost doubled its size and will facilitate processing of a whole new line of poultry products that are pre-cooked as convenience foods. The new line includes chicken nuggets, sausage, frankfurters, corn dogs, and fried chicken. Some of the precooked products are destined for export to Pacific Rim countries, where Hooley sees a whole

Edward Heyerly, founder of Willamette Poultry.

new market opening up. Among the 300 guests attending the opening of the addition was Governor Vic Atiyeh, who praised Willamette Poultry Co. for its success and cut the symbolic ribbon.

STRETCH & SEW, INC.

The business that mushroomed into the multimillion-dollar enterprise known nationwide as Stretch & Sew, Inc., began in 1966 with a Eugene housewife teaching teenage girls how to make cotton knit T-shirts. Now she's teaching the busy women of the 1980s how to sew everything from designer-look tees to a quilt ensemble for their homes—and helping them plan their wardrobes as well.

Ann Person, founder and president of Stretch & Sew, began experimenting with stretch knit fabric remnants, which resulted in the creation of basic sewing techniques and special patterns for this new material. Knits had not been generally available before, and there were no patterns or guidelines available for the home sewer. Ann began giving sewing lessons and women crowded the classes, eager to learn her methods. When she wasn't teaching, she was cutting her own patterns out of butcher paper and hand lettering them to sell to customers eager for easy patterns in multiple sizes that were suitable for knits.

In 1967 she opened the first Stretch & Sew Fabrics Center in Eugene, offering both classes and fabrics. By the end of 1968 she had five retail outlets and a wholesale operation to buy fabric directly from mills. In 1969 Stretch & Sew became a franchise operation, and by 1975 the firm was the official home-sewing authority for *Harper's Bazaar* magazine.

The 1980s had brought a new direction for Stretch & Sew. Fashionable patterns in multiple sizes that provide the easiest-ever approach to custom fitting are still the main emphasis of the company. Ann still designs and oversees the production of them. Only now the patterns are not only for knits but for woven fabrics as well. A

professional staff creates the patterns, then test sews and fits them on real people. Sewing instructions are developed and tested to make sure each pattern will turn out a professional-looking garment that rivals the best in ready-to-wear.

Ann's basic sewing book, first published in 1967 and updated through the years, has ultimately sold more than two million copies. Joining it is a new series of specialty books on lingerie, activewear, swimsuits, jackets, knit dressing, home decorating, wardrobe planning, color analysis, and quilting. Ann also wrote the first book on the market that dealt especially with sergers, the overlock machines that are revolutionizing the home-sewing industry.

The company has licensed stores

Ann Person, designer, teacher, host of her own TV show, mother, and grandmother, is the dynamic president of Stretch & Sew.

throughout the United States and Canada. In addition, it sells books and patterns, as well as providing a buying service and fashion forecasts, to independent fabric stores.

Stretch & Sew has changed through the years, but the lady who started it all has changed very little. She continues to be a dynamic force in the home-sewing industry, bringing the most up-to-date sewing methods to the consumer and presenting them in the most uncomplicated manner possible. She's still dedicated to the proposition that sewing should be fast, fun, and easy.

SWANSON BROTHERS LUMBER CO., INC.

Swanson-Superior Forest Products, Inc. (above left), and Swanson Brothers Lumber Co., Inc. (below right).

Alpha is the beginning, and it was in the tiny community of Alpha, Oregon, that Louis Swanson, a Swedish immigrant, settled with his family just before the turn of the century. Swanson raised Jersey cows, and his dairy farm was a success. However, Alpha represented more than just the beginning of a thriving family farm. Two of the homesteader's sons were to move from Deadwood Creek to Noti and begin what would become a multi-million-dollar lumber enterprise.

It was in 1937 that H.R. and Walter H. Swanson joined with Elvin May to form Swanson and May Lumber Co. H.R. had been a lumber inspector for the Southern Pacific Railroad for twenty-one years and Walter had been a logger; going into the lumber business seemed logical and in keeping with the family tradition of "being your own boss." With little capital, the partners bought pieces of machinery from an old mill and

moved them to Noti, where they bought some land, leased some more, and established their sawmill.

In 1945 May retired and the company name was changed to Swanson Brothers Lumber Co. When a group of investors from out of state purchased the firm in 1946 they retained the name, and the two brothers continued to manage the operation until 1948. When the brothers left the company, Ray Swanson, H.R.'s son and the mill's head sawyer, took over as manager. From the beginning, regardless of ownership, a Swanson has been running the mill.

It was fortuitous that the new owners did not change the company's name—because H.R. and Walt Swanson bought it back again in 1949. This time, however,

they were joined by Ray and by M.B. Marsh, the logging superintendent. They split the operation into two separate entities: Swanson Brothers Logging Co., Inc., a four-way corporation, and Swanson Brothers Lumber Co., Inc., a partnership.

Over the next two decades the firms grew, acquiring the 520-acre Triple Creek Ranch in 1950 and adding more timberlands each year. The 1950s and 1960s were busy years for the mill, which was turning out quantities of such specialty items as stadium seats for use across the country and decking for everything from aircraft carriers to Florida shrimp boats.

Both Marsh and H.R. Swanson retired from ownership in the late 1950s, and Ray became the sole proprietor in 1968 following Walt's death. Ray brought the two enterprises back under one corporate structure and in 1973 formed a separate concern, Swanson-Superior Forest Products, with two of his brothers and two Swanson Brothers Lumber shareholders, John Nail and Sam Konnie. The Swanson-Superior mill, which sits next to the original mill in Noti, is geared for smaller timber and does not make specialty products.

Swanson Brothers Lumber Co. was divided in 1984, with Ray Swanson taking most of the timberlands, and Sam Konnie retaining the sawmill.

Ray formed a new corporation for management of the 2,800 acres of timberland he oversees. He calls it Transition, Inc., an apt name for the culmination of a family-owned business that moved from a rickety sawmill, producing three million feet of lumber per year to a combined operation that in 1984 produced almost seventy million feet of lumber for export throughout the world.

SKEIE'S JEWELERS

ed a jewelry store with a partner who lent his last name, Dean, to that of Skeie for the store's name. Skeie sent for his girlfriend, Mamie, who had remained in Norway, and the two were married in Helena. The following year the Skeies and Dean moved to Round-up, Montana, where they opened another Dean and Skeie store.

After a brief stint in California in the early 1920s, Skeie heard that there was a small jewelry store for sale in Eugene and so he bought it. There was a thriving Scandinavian population in the area, and the green countryside

Skeie's downtown Eugene store is at 1027 Willamette Street.

In 1969 Skeie's Jewelers opened this second store in the Valley River Center.

Skeie's Jewelers traces its roots to Lars Skeie, a watchmaker in Voss, Norway, in the 1800s. Lars had two sons, Gustaf and Ole, who also were certified watchmakers, and it is thanks to Ole that Eugene has two Skeie's Jewelers stores today.

Ole Skeie came to the United States in 1907 and worked in a Chicago jewelry house for the next two years. In 1909 he moved to Forsyth, Montana, where he start-

and the forests reminded Skeie of Norway. That first Skeie's store in Eugene, at 927 Willamette Street, measured only fifteen feet by thirty feet, but it was a start.

In 1935 Rex Hamaker married Skeie's daughter, Lucille, and entered into business with his father-

in-law. Clark Fee, a watchmaker and bench jeweler, also joined the firm in the mid-1940s, and Skeie's moved to larger quarters at 1027 Willamette. In 1947 Ole's son, George, returned with his wife, Mabel, to Eugene from Salt Lake City, where he had been an optometrist. George set up an optometry shop in the back of the store and practiced there for the next five years.

Over the next two decades ownership of Skeie's Jewelers changed hands but it did not leave the family—it simply worked its way through succeeding generations. George Skeie bought Clark Fee's interest in the company in 1950, and Rex Hamaker's death in 1965 left a substantial portion of his ownership to George and a portion to his wife, Lucille, George's sister. From Ole Skeie's children, the store passed on to his grandchildren. Stephen Hamaker, son of Rex and Lucy, purchased his mother's share in the business in 1967; Richard Skeie, son of George and Mabel who had come into the business in 1975, joined Steve in buying out his father's share in 1979; and Michael McNutt, whose mother, Norma, was another of Ole Skeie's daughters, became manager of the downtown store in 1981.

Rick Skeie and Steve Hamaker are partners today in an operation that their grandfather could hardly have dreamed of when he opened his first shop in Eugene in 1922. In 1969 Skeie's Jewelers opened a second store at Valley River Center and the firm now has more than thirty employees, including two watchmakers, three bench jewelers, and three gemologists. Both stores specialize in fine jewelry and are carrying on the family tradition of expert craftsmanship begun by Ole's father, Lars, so long ago in Norway.

SPECTRA-PHYSICS LASER SYSTEMS DIVISION

When the checker at the super-market electronically "beeps" the price of a can of beans into a register rather than ringing it up manually, chances are that the Spectra-Physics Laser Systems Division in Eugene has had a hand in the process. In 1961, when Spectra-Physics was formed, scientists were only beginning to explore the characteristics and potential applications of laser light. Using the gas laser as a source of intense and visible light, Spectra focused on new research applications.

Initially, the corporation grew through acquisition; it purchased University Labs in 1969 and Autolab in 1972. But when Spectra formed its Electronic Label Reader Division in 1973, it was developing a new product and a new market without the benefit of experience that an acquired company can offer.

By late summer a team of twenty people were working around the clock to develop a laser-beam optical scanning system. The first scanners were sent to the annual

Spectra-Physics Laser Systems Division pioneered the development of laser scanners for supermarket point-of-sale applications. Pictured here is a slot scanner.

Spectra-Physics Laser Systems Division in Eugene is a multinational, multimillion-dollar supplier of lasers and bar-code-reading equipment.

convention of the Food Marketing Institute in May 1974. Spectra-Physics displayed twelve of the fifteen scanners there, and the scanners' performance clearly positioned Spectra as an industry leader.

In June 1974 the first totally electronic supermarket using Universal Product Code symbols on merchandise became operational. Marsh Supermarkets in Troy, Ohio, installed an NCR system with a Spectra-Physics laser scanner. Two months later Spectra signed a contract to supply NCR with scanners over the next two years. Initially, demand for the new technology was slowed by customer resistance to the removal of traditional price display and by employee concerns over potential job loss. This fear was allayed as people became comfortable with the system's integrity and the productivity that it achieved.

As a result, Spectra-Physics maintained a strong interest in scanners and in 1979 decided to

build a facility in Eugene to produce them. Twenty engineers and support personnel moved to the area in early 1980 and within one year the new facility employed 250 people. Although the business had its ups and downs through the early 1980s, today it is a multinational, multimillion-dollar supplier of lasers and bar-code-reading equipment.

Spectra continued its research and development activities over the years and has focused on diversifying its product line. In 1983 two new products were developed—the SP2001 hand-held scanner and the flat-top, point-of-sale scanner. In 1984 employment at the Eugene plant reached 400, and plans were being finalized for expansion, including an additional building on the site.

Spectra-Physics Laser Systems Division, which pioneered the development of laser scanners for supermarket point-of-sale applications in the early 1970s, has turned that pioneering spirit to Eugene's advantage. Today the firm is a prime beneficiary of an international increase in demand for all types of bar-code-reading devices, and Eugene is a beneficiary of the positive effects engendered by a high-technology corporation that holds a leadership position in a fast-growing industry.

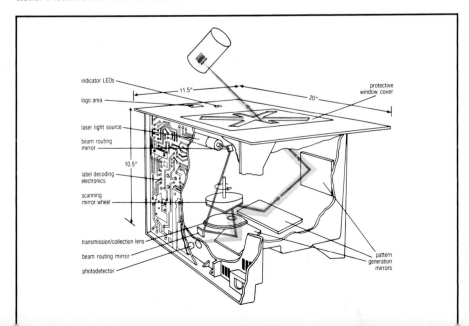

indicator LEDs

logo area

laser light source

beam routing mirror

label decoding electronics

scanning mirror wheel

transmission/collection lens

beam routing mirror

photodetector

11.5"

20"

10.5"

protective window cover

pattern generation mirrors

145

WILDISH GROUP OF COMPANIES

Fifty years ago Thomas C. Wildish, his wife, Verna, and ten of their children loaded into the family's car and pickup truck and headed for Oregon from their farm in the drought-stricken plains of North Dakota. They did not realize that this move was the first step toward the founding of a multimillion-dollar organization that would bear the family name, and play an integral role in the growth and development of the Eugene-Springfield community.

When the family arrived in Eugene, T.C. Wildish traded his pickup truck for a dump truck and began hauling sand and gravel. The delivery business prospered, and by 1941 Wildish owned twelve trucks and was hauling sand and gravel all over the state. The trucks operated out of a shed at the north end of High Street in Eugene, where they were driven during the day, and repaired at night.

During the war years the firm acquired a bulldozer and excavating equipment and branched out from simply hauling materials to doing excavation and underground utility work. The company's first construction job was as a subcontractor, but soon Wildish was bidding independently on underground utility work. The firm also was involved in military and government work during the war, including hauling aggregate for Fern Ridge Dam.

In 1945 T.C. Wildish Co. bought its first plant site at 5001 Franklin Boulevard in the Glenwood area. That was the beginning of the acquisition of sand and gravel land along the Coast and Middle forks of the Willamette River, which eventually led to the ownership of more than 1,000 acres in the Mt. Pisgah area. In the postwar years, though, development of plant op-

erations was as important to the firm's future as was land acquisition. Wildish built its own gravel crushing plant in 1947 and was, for the first time, in a position to furnish its own materials.

The company purchased a small asphalt plant in 1951 and put it to a rigorous test the next year, when Wildish contracted with the City of Springfield to do the bulk of the paving work between Twenty-first and Twenty-eighth streets and from Main to E streets. The plant produced twenty tons per hour, requiring Wildish to buy asphalt

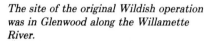
The site of the original Wildish operation was in Glenwood along the Willamette River.

from another supplier in order to keep up with the job. With as many as four asphalt plants producing between 250-300 tons per hour each in recent years, that first major contracting job has become an amusing memory.

The 1950s brought a gradual expansion in the volume of business, with a concentration on paving

Wildish served as the general contractor for the Barker Stadium Club facility that is attached to Autzen Stadium at the University of Oregon.

This shovel, with its eight-cubic-yard bucket, is used to dig sand and gravel at the firm's McKenzie River plant site. Standing, from left, are Thomas E. Wildish, chairman of the board and chief executive officer; Leonard A. Wildish, director; and Norman E. Wildish, vice-chairman. Kneeling, from left, are Gary A. Wildish, vice-president; Richard E. Wildish, president; and James A. Wildish, vice-president.

and utility work in subdivisions and on city contracts for the resurfacing of streets. In 1959 Wildish Sand and Gravel Co. was incorporated. Steadily, the various Wildish activities were increasing the corporation's ability to provide the manpower, expertise, and materials for the work the organization was doing, which paid off in efficiency and cost effectiveness.

And efficiency was the key word in 1968, when Wildish was named the prime contractor for resurfacing and building up the runway at Eugene's Mahlon Sweet Airport. The airport had to be closed because of the runway's deteriorated condition, and Wildish coordinated the efforts and mix designs of two other sand and gravel firms in order to achieve maximum construction speed. For three weeks seemingly endless lines of dump trucks filed out to the airport, where men and machines got the

runway into shape.

Throughout the 1960s and 1970s the Wildish enterprises grew in both scope and physical size as additional plants and land were acquired in Eugene, Corvallis, and Medford. During those years the firm left its imprint on virtually every street in Eugene and Springfield, and it also participated in the construction of freeways and logging roads.

Having entered the concrete production business in 1959, the firm began concrete construction work in the 1970s. Beginning with work on foundations for sawmills and concrete machinery bases, experience was quickly gained and by the latter part of the decade the company became the prime contractor for the Glenwood solid-waste transfer station. It also did much of the excavation work and provided concrete for Eugene's downtown mall, the Hult Center, and the regional sewage treatment plant.

Today Wildish Land Co. is involved in full-scale building construction and land development activities. For example, the firm served as general contractor for the Autzen Stadium clubhouse for the University of Oregon and has developed its own industrial park and coastal residential subdivision.

Wildish has continued expanding

its geographic market area during the past few years, constructing a research facility in Bend and a $5.5-million office in Salem, doing reconstruction work on the Redwood Highway in Northern California, and handling concrete construction in central Washington for a silicon-chip manufacturing plant. Wildish has an office and construction equipment in Mesa, Arizona, as well, but Lane County is still home for this family operation.

Thomas C. Wildish died in 1963, but his family and many close associates have carried on the traditions he established. Today the third generation of the Wildish family is involved in the business that began with a single truck and has grown into a multifaceted construction firm proud of its reputation as a "one-source" contractor.

Thomas C. Wildish, founder.

Part of the firm's fleet as it appeared in the late 1950s.

NORTHWEST SYSTEMS

Wayne L. Johnson, founder of Northwest Systems.

When Wayne L. Johnson got out of the Army in 1954, he was looking for a place to start his career. Johnson, who had grown up in Idaho and served in Germany as deputy finance officer with the 1st Infantry Division, graduated with a degree in business and accounting from Northwest Nazarene College in Idaho. He saw economic potential in the Northwest and was particularly drawn to Eugene because it offered fishing, hunting, skiing, and white-water floating, in addition to the cultural amenities that resulted from the presence of the University of Oregon.

With his decision to settle in Eugene made, Johnson began developing the talents and contacts that over the next thirty-one years would result in the founding of many enterprises, Foremost Investment, Inc., a personal holding company; Foremost Construction Company; many limited partnerships; and Northwest Systems, a commercial real estate investment and syndication firm. However, the transition from being an under-financed ex-GI looking for work to being the owner of Lane County's largest real estate investment firm, handling millions of dollars in transactions annually, was a gradual one.

Johnson's first job in Eugene was with Olsen and Quick, a market and restaurant equipment company. Johnson soon bought out Quick, and the firm's name became Olsen and Johnson Equipment Company. He later bought out Olsen as well, merging that company with Central Restaurant Supply, later selling his interest in the firm. That same year Johnson founded Foremost Investments and Foremost Construction Company.

During his years as a developer and builder in the Eugene-Spring-field area, Johnson built more than 1,500 apartment units and was a managing partner in the majority of them. He also designed and equipped the Timber Topper restaurant in Springfield, whose owner then embarked on the King's Table, a national restaurant chain. Since then, Johnson has built numerous restaurants for independent and chain operations, including Shakey's Pizza Parlors and Popeye's Fried Chicken restaurants. Johnson and his companies were involved in major retail developments as well, the largest being the eighteen-acre Bear Creek Shopping Center in Medford, which was built and syndicated in 1979.

Since that time Johnson's business emphasis has shifted, as reflected by the formation in 1980 of Northwest Systems-Real Estate Investments. The firm, wholly owned by Johnson, deals with the listing and selling of investment properties, and the formation of syndications. Northwest Systems sold more than forty-five million dollars in investment properties in 1984 and expects to do better each subsequent year. With a staff of seven consultants, whose areas of expertise range from real estate investment to mortgage brokering and insurance needs, Northwest Systems today conducts business in such cities as Seattle, Portland, Los Angeles, and the western half of the United States.

But the company remains headquartered in Eugene, and Johnson has maintained an interest in the community affairs of the town he adopted as his permanent home thirty-one years ago. Today Johnson is a great booster of Eugene-Springfield development, and an aggressive promoter of both economic and high-technology growth.

THE FOGELSTROM CO.

Norman J. Fogelstrom, at the Fifth Street Public Market building in Eugene.

Norman Fogelstrom hadn't really planned to be a developer, or a building designer, or an architectural innovator, but he wound up being all three. He majored in business at the University of Oregon and in 1961 went into mortgage banking. Three years later he joined the real estate department of what is now First Interstate Bank, dealing primarily in mortgage loans. But Fogelstrom was interested in more than financing structures—he was interested in building them.

In 1967 Fogelstrom and two architect friends decided to try their hand at the residential development field. The idea was to design basic house plans and develop a few different models. But Fogelstrom didn't like the plans the architects were coming up with and began designing his own. He was soon in business for himself.

The Fogelstrom Co. originally operated out of a trailer on a fif-

teen-lot subdivision, but it was no "cookie-cutter" construction project. After the first house was presold on a to-be-designed basis, Fogelstrom changed the firm's approach; every house would be custom designed and built. Fogelstrom designed and constructed some 200 private residences, including about 40 percent of the custom-built larger homes in Eugene, until 1979, when he devoted himself exclusively to commercial building.

Fogelstrom had begun doing commercial work in 1969, including some of the downtown mall stores, dental and medical buildings, restaurants, warehouses, and office buildings. But in 1975 he began to play around with the idea of something completely different for Eugene: a public market. He and his wife, Donna, had been impressed

with public markets in Seattle, San Francisco, Boston, and other cities, and they felt Eugene was ready for one. Fogelstrom took an option on an old packing plant used for storage at the corner of Fifth and High streets and began tentative designs.

What was to become the Fifth Street Public Market opened in 1976 as a single-story structure, housing retail shops and such innovative designs as a "food court," which brought into a single open area food vendors and unsegregated dining space. The project was an immediate success. With Donna Fogelstrom as leasing agent, the market soon had more tenants than it had space, and plans for expansion seemed inevitable.

In 1978 Fogelstrom bought the contiguous lot to the west and tore down an existing granary and incubator structure. The following year the couple formed a partnership with Obie Communication, Inc., to enable further expansion of the Fifth Street Public Market.

Plans for the completed market, designed by Fogelstrom, included a building of about 300,000 square feet, housing office as well as retail space and featuring courtyards, promenades, and skylights. However, in 1979 the changing economic climate forced postponement of that plan, and in 1980 work began on a more modest addition. It opened in 1981, bringing the market to its present size.

Although The Fogelstrom Co. has most recently been involved in developing a covered shopping mall in Corvallis and although the Fogelstrom stamp is on some of Eugene's most prestigious homes, Norman Fogelstrom is best known as the fellow who played Pygmalion with a downtown warehouse and put some pizzazz in the Eugene shopping experience.

111

ZELLNER PROPERTIES

George L. Zellner was born and raised on a farm in Washington, and he fully expected to be a farmer, which he became. He did not, however, expect to be an oatmeal manufacturer or an exotic cattle importer or a land developer—all of which he also became.

Zellner came to Eugene in 1941, bringing the sawmill he had owned and operated in Washington. Private timberlands in Washington were disappearing rapidly, but there was still plenty of timber in Oregon for an independent mill.

The Zellner Lumber Corporation employed as many as 235 workers at one point and operated in Eugene until Zellner sold it to Eugene Stud & Veneer Company in 1955. But the sale of the Eugene lumber mill did not mean Zellner was getting out of the lumber business; on the contrary, in 1957 he bought a half-interest in Zel-Loney Lumber Company at Coquille and an interest in Mt. Baldy Lumber Company in Yoncalla. That same year he started the Zellner Lumber Corporation in Kooskie, Idaho.

He did not move from Eugene, however, and for seventeen years he commuted fifty times per year in his plane between his home and his business in Kooskie. In the latter part of the 1950s he also bought a half-interest in a lumber mill in Bozeman, Montana.

In 1956 Zellner had formed Zellner Properties, a family partnership owned by himself and his wife, Emily, to manage his ever-

George L. Zellner, owner of Zellner Properties.

growing investments. He fulfilled his youthful ambition in 1960 when he bought Brightoaks, a farm of about 1,000 acres between Coburg and Harrisburg. Although he had most recently been in the lumber business, Zellner had taught agriculture in a Washington high school in the early 1930s and had come from a farming family.

At Brightoaks, however, he turned his attention to cattle, and throughout the early 1960s he bred European beef cattle, including breeds from Italy, Switzerland, and France. With 1,000 head, Zellner was the largest breeder of European continental cattle on the Pacific Coast and one of the ten largest in the country.

It was also in 1960 that Zellner became involved in the publishing business as a partner in Industrial Publishers of Eugene. The firm publishes industrial catalogs and auction brochures for distribution throughout North America.

That same year the Four Corners shopping center, with George Zellner as sole owner, developer, and builder, opened for business. Zellner had bought the land, formerly used as a feedlot, in 1946 and had maintained his office there. The Four Corners property was one of many Zellner developments, both commercial and residential, throughout the region over the years. Locally, he developed some eighty acres of the Panorama View area in Eugene's South Hills and has developed other properties in Beaverton, Redmond, Medford, and Coos Bay.

In 1965 Zellner started Coast Manufacturing, at one time the largest manufacturer of solid pine shelving in the United States. The plant is still operating, but today makes pine module shelving to fit on metal structures. Coast Manufacturing has produced storeroom

shelving for JCPenney's; Sears, Roebuck, and Co.; Montgomery Ward's; and K mart stores nationwide.

In addition to manufacturing, milling, and land developing, Zellner had also started an equipment-liquidating business called the Machinery Exchange. It was through the Machinery Exchange that Zellner found himself, in 1960, with what had been a feed mill and egg-processing plant.

He liquidated the equipment but was left with the building, and several years later, when he bought Triangle Cereal Company in Portland, he moved the equipment into the old mill and began making oatmeal. Today Triangle Cereal, with its distinctive silos bearing the Zellner Milling name, is one of only five oatmeal plants in the country and is the largest user of oats on the West Coast.

Indeed, the cereal mill has become Zellner Properties' largest operation, producing sixteen tons of oatmeal per day and exporting to as far away as the Orient. The mill rolls oats for both instant and regular oatmeal, but only the regular variety is sold in retail stores. In addition, the mill rolls oats for use in rodent poisoning, although the poison is added elsewhere.

Today Zellner is experimenting on his farm with organically grown oats and wheat for rolling, although he does not use his own crops in his mill. Grain grown without the aid of pesticides is difficult to find, and Zellner is anticipating a market in the region's health food stores. It seems logical and fitting that, despite the great diversity of Zellner Properties over the years, George Zellner—who always thought he'd be a farmer—should, in his seventieth year, be growing natural grains at Brightoaks.

McKENZIE-WILLAMETTE HOSPITAL

Early in the 1900s residents of Springfield faced a host of dreaded and life-threatening diseases common to that time—everything from smallpox to polio—yet most medicine was still practiced in individual homes by private physicians. The Springfield Private Hospital was converted into a boarding-house in 1914 and was replaced by Springfield General Hospital, which was converted into apartments in 1936. It was not until after World War II that residents of Springfield and nearby communities began seriously discussing the need for—and the possibility of—a first-rate, full-service hospital.

In 1949 the McKenzie-Willamette Hospital Association was formed, and from that beginning grew the multimillion-dollar, modern health care facility that today includes a helicopter landing pad atop a state-of-the-art Ancillary Building housing support services, a ten-bed intensive care unit, and a whole-body CT scanner. But all of this was far beyond the dreams of the first nine-member board of directors, whose primary task it was to raise funds for a modest but modern hospital to serve the community. Professional fund raisers and some 3,500 volunteers went to work, and on October 30, 1953, a victory banquet was held to celebrate their efforts; a sufficient number of pledges had been received to guarantee a modern, 35-bed hospital.

Just over a year later McKenzie-Willamette Hospital opened its doors at 1460 G Street. The first expansion of the original single-story building was made in 1957, when a laundry, maintenance shop, and conference room were added. Further small additions, primarily built with hospital-generated funds and federal grants, were made through the 1960s, including an

McKenzie-Willamette Hospital is located at 1460 G Street in Springfield.

emergency department, a new business office, laboratory, expanded radiology and physical therapy departments, and an intensive coronary care unit.

But despite this expansion, by 1971 the community was well on its way to outgrowing its hospital. Doctors reported scheduling problems in the two operating rooms, the dietary department needed more space, and beds were sometimes set up in the corridors when there were more patients than there were rooms. After an extensive study of the problem, the board decided on a long-range expansion plan, and a community fund drive was once again implemented to provide some of the funding for the proposed $4.5-million construction program. The resulting four-story addition housed larger dietary facilities, new operating rooms, central supply areas, and a 36-bed nursing floor.

By 1980 overcrowding was again a problem, with several of the institution's departments having increased in size by more than 50 percent. Hospital officials requested and received permission to build a $16.5-million ancillary facility, and the McKenzie-Willamette Hospital Development Council was formed to help finance it. The development council, made up entirely of community volunteers, ultimately raised $1.1 million as a down payment on the new facility.

In October 1983, thirty years after that first victory celebration marking sufficient pledges to begin construction on the institution, McKenzie-Willamette Hospital held another celebration—this one to dedicate a state-of-the-art facility designed to provide full

and efficient patient care. The 72,000-square-foot Ancillary Building includes a new radiology department, day-surgery unit, emergency room, intensive care unit, and, of course, the helipad for emergency cases brought in by helicopter.

Throughout its history when McKenzie-Willamette Hospital needed to expand, it turned—appropriately enough—to the community for help. The ties between the institution and the community have been strong since those days in the late 1940s, when members of the community began working toward the idea of a local hospital. McKenzie-Willamette has strengthened those ties through community outreach programs that take health care outside the traditional confines of the hospital room through health care education.

Typical classes at the institution include instruction in cardiopulmonary resuscitation, a baby-sitting skills course for sixth and seventh

graders, and a prenatal education course for expectant parents. In addition, doctors and other health care professionals routinely offer seminars open to the public for discussion of such topics as stress, common childhood illnesses, sports injuries, and depression. Other nontraditional approaches stress preventive health care, such as the walking-for-exercise clinic sponsored by the hospital and clinics on self-examination for breast cancer.

With its trained staff of health care professionals, its physical growth, and acquisition of the newest in health care equipment, McKenzie-Willamette Hospital has more than met the hopes and dreams of those citizens who over thirty years ago spearheaded the effort to develop a local facility to serve the community.

The hospital's Ancillary Building houses support services, a ten-bed intensive care unit, and a whole-body CT scanner.

INTERNATIONAL KING'S TABLE

Wilbur Houmes (center) and two unidentified workers behind the counter of Willie's Sandwich Shop, 956 Oak Street, in 1950.

When young Wilbur Houmes was selling five- and ten-cent hamburgers at the Blue Bell Sandwich Shop in Eugene in the early 1940s, he had no way of knowing that this was only the first small step in a career that would ultimately find him at the head of a multimillion-dollar restaurant chain serving patrons nationwide.

Houmes had been born and reared on a farm in South Dakota, but the 1930s brought droughts, and Houmes escaped the Dust Bowl in 1934, just after his high school graduation, by moving west to Oregon. His brother had moved to the area around Drain in 1930, and Houmes joined him there. He spent a year cutting wood and hunting, and later worked with the Civilian Conservation Corps. In 1936 he married his high school sweetheart, who came to Oregon from South Dakota, and the following year Wilbur and Elna Houmes moved to Eugene.

At that time jobs were hard to find in Eugene, but in 1940 Houmes became a dishwasher and then a waiter at the Blue Bell Sandwich Shop at 956 Oak Street. After the war he opened his own restaurant, a ten-stool lunch counter called Willie's Chili Bowl, at 125 East Broadway. The lunch counter was a success, and in 1949 Houmes sold it and bought the Blue Bell Sandwich Shop, which he operated as Willie's Sandwich Shop.

Through the years Houmes was gaining experience and expertise in the food-service business, and in 1957, a year after he sold the sandwich shop, he opened the Timber Topper restaurant in Springfield, with a dining room seating about sixty-five and a drive-in in the back. The Timber Topper opened in July to fairly good trade, but a recession in the fall forced Houmes to try something different to attract customers—a buffet.

In January 1958 Houmes began offering a fixed-price buffet dinner one or two nights a week. It was a tremendous success, and by the end of February the Timber Topper offered buffet lunches and dinners every day. With a low fixed price and a variety of hot and cold

A typical King's Table restaurant, this is one of eighty-one in operation. Two are in Lane County, one in Springfield and the other in Eugene.

foods, the restaurant was packed most of the time, and in 1959 Houmes enlarged the dining room to seat more than 100.

In 1964 Houmes organized Timber Topper, Inc., and opened a Timber Topper buffet in Salem. It was an immediate success and in 1965 was expanded to 270 seats. The large number of out-of-towners who stopped at both Timber Topper restaurants while on vacation gave Houmes the idea of franchising his operation. In 1966, under the name of International King's Table, he began franchising through a Chicago organization.

The following year Houmes' son, Roger, who had been in the Army, returned from Germany and joined the corporation as manager of the Salem restaurant. Later that year he became vice-president of operations. Timber Topper, Inc., went public in 1968, with an offering of stock within the state of Oregon. At the same time the firm was merged with International King's Table and took that name.

The 1970s represented a major

growth period for King's Table. At the beginning of the decade the corporation owned and operated seven restaurants and had annual sales of $1.1 million. By the end of the decade it was operating fifty-four units, and sales exceeded thirty million dollars. King's Table opened a restaurant in Eugene at Oakway Mall in 1970, one on Mohawk Boulevard in Springfield 1972, and another on West Eleventh Avenue in Eugene in 1974. The Oakway restaurant later became Oh Susannah's, a subsidiary of King's Table.

The corporation was no longer in the franchising business by the end of the 1970s, having had up to twenty franchises—primarily in Kentucky, Indiana, and Tennessee—that were eventually bought out by the franchisees. Instead, King's Table was concentrating on expanding its chain of quality corporation-owned buffet restaurants, and in 1977 had a public offering of stock nationwide. Roger Houmes became president of the firm in 1978, although his father

remained chairman of the board of directors until his retirement in 1981.

The younger Houmes, who grew up around his father's restaurants and began working in the business at the age of fifteen, has continued the family tradition of providing good food at reasonable prices in a buffet setting. In 1983 King's Table bought out the Royal Fork chain of buffet restaurants, bringing to more than eighty the number of International King's Table restaurants throughout the western United States.

Such innovations as a senior citizens' discount program that offers special bargains for members have made King's Table particularly popular with older patrons, and the informal atmosphere and diversity of offerings have made the restaurants popular among young families as well. Today International King's Table still stresses the quality of good food properly prepared and attractively presented that made the first buffet a hit almost thirty years ago.

DUNHAM CADILLAC-OLDSMOBILE, INC.

Downtown Eugene looked a bit different when W.W. "Win" Dunham decided to give up his position as an Oldsmobile zone manager in Portland and open a Cadillac-Olds dealership in Eugene. The year was 1954, and Dunham's first showroom was on the site of the present city hall. The staff numbered twenty-four, including young Robert E. Brooke, a partner in the firm, who had married Dunham's daughter, Dorothy.

In September 1954, some three months after it opened for business, Dunham Motors moved to a larger facility at Thirteenth Avenue and Oak Street. Over the next few years the operation expanded until by 1959 it took up the entire square block from Willamette to Oak Street on Thirteenth Avenue. "Cadillac Corner" for used Cadillacs was established on the northeast corner, and D&B leasing and used cars was added on Thirteenth Avenue.

In 1959 Dunham Motors incorporated under the name Dunham Olds Cadillac, with Win Dunham as president and Robert Brooke as secretary/treasurer. Over the next decade the business grew and so

did the town. By the early 1970s Dunham Olds Cadillac was employing about forty people, including young Robert L. Brooke, who worked in the parts department and as a car washer at his father's dealership.

Development of the downtown mall created a need for a more desirable traffic pattern around the dealership, which also needed more room to grow. As a result, in 1972 Dunham Olds Cadillac moved to a five-acre site at 345 Goodpasture Island Road in the now-burgeoning Valley River area. The new location, its present site, provided ample room for the various firms that make up the corporation.

The companies include a finance department, the new car sales department, used car sales, a complete body shop, a parts department, an insurance department, and lease and service departments. The new car showroom doubled in size in 1981, the same year the dealership took on the Isuzu line. Isuzu, an independent Japanese automaker of which General Motors owns one-third, is Japan's largest producer of trucks.

Meanwhile, Dunham Olds Cadillac was making a name for itself in

In 1972 Dunham Olds Cadillac moved to a five-acre site at 345 Goodpasture Island Road. This location provides ample room for the various firms that make up the corporation.

the community and throughout the Northwest. The dealership routinely has provided vehicles for charitable causes and nonprofit groups, aiding everyone from local service organizations such as the Elks to the University of Oregon athletic department. Regionally, the dealership wins awards among its peers; year after year it has been one of only two dealerships to receive the Olds Service Merit Award for its zone, which includes Oregon, Washington, Alaska, western Idaho, and western Montana.

By the 1980s the corporation's management had undergone a subtle change. Win Dunham died in 1978, leaving Robert E. Brooke as president. Brooke's son, Robert L. Brooke, became secretary/treasurer, and his daughter, Terri, now works in the parts department. And there is a fourth generation waiting in the wings. Robert L. Brooke has two sons, too young to sell cars or repair engines yet, but then, their father started at the age of fourteen.

NORTHWEST NATURAL GAS COMPANY

Northwest Natural Gas Company, which brings efficient natural gas to the Eugene-Springfield area as well as other communities throughout Oregon and Washington, traces its roots to the gas franchise granted by the Oregon Territorial Legislature in 1859 to H.C. Leonard and John Green.

Their partnership had begun in Astoria, where the two operated a mercantile business. Leonard and Green decided that Portland was ripe for a gas lighting business, and in 1860 they purchased the necessary machinery and operated the Northwest's first manufactured gas plant using carbonized coal.

Only San Francisco and Sacramento had been operating gas plants on the West Coast, while New York had been using gas lighting for thirty-one years.

The founders' brothers, Henry Green and Irving Leonard, became partners in the company, and in 1862 the gasworks of the Leonard and Green Company was incorporated as the Portland Gas Light Company, with the four-way partnership retaining ownership and Henry Green as president.

The first recorded local use of gas for any purpose other than lighting was in 1868, when the City of Portland made arrangements with the company for keeping the water hot in the boilers of the

city's horse-drawn steam fire engines.

Sold to a group of businessmen in 1892, Portland Gas Light Company was renamed Portland Gas & Coke Company (Gasco), the modern beginning of what is now Northwest Natural Gas Company.

In the early part of the century, the electric light bulb posed a real threat to the natural gas industry, which relied on gas lighting for much of its revenues. But the invention of the gas range, furnace, and water heater provided opportunities for growth in the residential market. In the 1930s Gasco was serving more than 90,000 customers, and by 1946 over 110,000 area residents used gas. Over the years Gasco expanded its service territory with mergers and the con-

Gasco customer servicemen, some still wearing World War I uniforms, traveled on motorcycles in 1919.

struction of new gas lines.

Eugene joined the Gasco family after the company acquired the territory from Cascade Natural Gas Corporation in 1958. Its petroleum-air gas distribution served approximately 1,300 customers in Eugene and Springfield. That same year Portland Gas & Coke Company changed its name to Northwest Natural Gas Company after converting much of its system to natural gas.

The Eugene area obtains its natural gas from a network of pipelines running from Camas, Washington, down the Willamette Valley, through Eugene to Medford and Grants Pass.

Now serving more than 266,000 customers system-wide, Northwest Natural Gas Company continues to serve a growing industrial and residential market in the Eugene-Springfield area, providing efficient energy at the lowest possible price.

This October 1923 photo is of the Linnton plant, where gas was manufactured from 1913 to 1956.

DUTCH GIRL ICE CREAM

In 1938 the six Gustafson brothers, Kenneth, Elmer, Claus, Oliver, Reuben, and Melvin, put up fifty dollars each to start an ice cream shop in Cottage Grove, Oregon. This was the beginning of the Gustafson family's association with ice cream—an association that has grown and prospered for more than forty-five years and shows every indication of continuing through future generations.

The brothers maintained the Cottage Grove ice cream shop and in 1939 bought Dutch Girl Dairy in Eugene, a small home-delivery milk company. They sold the milk route, bought a five-gallon freezer for making ice cream, and converted the enterprise, at 1224 Willamette, into a restaurant-dairy store. Their Dutch Girl Ice Cream became so popular that in 1941 they built an ice cream plant behind the restaurant and began wholesaling ice cream to local stores.

By the end of World War II Claus and Kenneth had sold their interests in the business. Reuben died in 1943 and his wife, Ethel, became a partner in the firm and served as office manager. After the war Dutch Girl entered the frozen-food business as a distributor, and by 1955 it had a fleet of six trucks—two refrigerated—and was delivering frozen products

In 1940 this truck represented Dutch Girl's entire fleet.

throughout the Willamette Valley.

However, ice cream has always been the mainstay of Dutch Girl. In 1955 the firm moved to its present location at Eighth and Grant streets and has continued to expand its facilities and upgrade equipment over the intervening years. The facility today is 2.5 times larger than the original plant, and ice cream production has increased from twenty gallons per hour at the beginning of 1955 to 1,200 gallons per hour in 1985.

In the early 1970s Dutch Girl expanded its marketplace to southern Oregon and in 1974 joined Quality Chekd, a national association of dairy product wholesalers. Aided by that national-brand rec-

ognition, Dutch Girl is now distributed in Washington, Northern California, and Alaska.

The firm has also expanded almost yearly in terms of plant size and volume since the late 1960s. In 1969 a new building was added for freezer storage space, and there have been two major expansions of freezer space since then. The addition in 1982 of a plate hardener for flash freezing increased potential ice cream volume from one million to three million gallons per year.

Yet through growth, expansion, and diversification, one thing at Dutch Girl has not changed—it is still a family operation. Gene Gustafson, son of Ethel and Reuben, began working for the company in 1948 and became a partner in 1957. He became owner in 1974 and brought his two sons, Mike and Mark, into the business. With Mrs. Ethel Gustafson still working at the Dutch Girl office, three generations are actively involved in a multimillion-dollar enterprise that began with a five-gallon freezer and a storefront restaurant almost fifty years ago.

Today the firm has seven trucks, and Dutch Girl products are distributed in Washington, Northern California, and Alaska.

EUGENE WATER & ELECTRIC BOARD

Eugene's municipal water and electric utility was formed shortly after a typhoid fever epidemic was traced to the privately owned water system that served the town at the turn of the century. Following a citizen vote, the city took over the private water system in 1908 and ordered construction of a hydroelectric project along the McKenzie River to provide the power needed to pump water at adequate pressure and for street lighting. On March 11, 1911, less than a month following completion of the Walterville Hydroelectric Plant, the city turned over control of the municipal utilities to a separate board of five commissioners. The Eugene Water Board, as it was called until the name was changed to Eugene Water & Electric Board in 1949, was made independent of city government to assure that the utility revenues would not be used for other city purposes.

The Walterville Plant produced surplus electricity that the board sold in competition with a private power company. The number of electric customers grew from two on December 1, 1911, to 1,001 twelve months later. Its first customer, Eugene Planing Mill, is still a customer today. The utility purchased the private power company in 1916 to become the sole electricity supplier in Eugene.

In 1927 the utility switched from the Willamette River to the McKenzie River for the source of Eugene's water supply. The Hayden Bridge Filtration Plant was completed in 1950 near the river northeast of Springfield. Water from the plant exceeds all standards for water quality, and the plant has been expanded to easily handle the area's water needs.

The need for electricity has grown with the community. A second McKenzie River hydroelectric project was built near Leaburg in 1930. An oil-fired steam plant was built in 1931 and wood-fired boilers were added in 1942 and 1950. (The steam plant today provides process steam for downtown-area buildings and businesses and is not used to generate electricity.) The utility's largest generating plant, the Carmen-Smith Project in the Cascade Range east of Eugene, was

The Eugene Water & Electric Board offices are located between the Ferry Street overpass and the Willamette River. Adjacent to the offices, hogged fuel (wood waste) is stored for burning in the EWEB steam plant (the building on the left next to the river).

completed in 1963. A cogeneration plant was built in 1976 at the Weyerhaeuser Corporation in Springfield. The plant uses excess steam produced by Weyerhaeuser's operations to drive an EWEB-owned turbine-generator. EWEB's projects today meet about one-fourth of the community's electricity needs. EWEB gets most of its electricity supply from the federal Bonneville Power Administration.

Today EWEB is a leader in providing energy conservation services for its customers and has researched renewable energy resources such as geothermal, small hydro, wind, and solar energy for possible future development.

Still governed by an independent, five-member, citizen-elected board whose members serve without pay, EWEB is proud of its heritage as a publicly owned utility that places highest priority on providing excellent service at low cost. The utility has never needed taxpayer support. In fact, it pays several million dollars each year "in lieu of taxes" to the city and other local governments.

Since 1911 Eugene Water & Electric Board has been a major contributor to the health, prosperity, and quality of life in Eugene.

EWEB purifies the community's water supply at the Hayden Bridge Filtration Plant. After treatment at the plant, the McKenzie River water exceeds all quality standards.

MYRMO & SONS, INC.

George Myrmo and his wife, Olga, brought a truckload of blacksmith's tools and their three children, Helga, Arthur, and Emil, to Eugene from Glendale, Oregon, in 1925. Myrmo began his shop, named simply George Myrmo: Blacksmith, on a 50- by 150-foot lot at 1937 Franklin Boulevard, then on the outskirts of Eugene. With Olga occasionally helping out in the office, Myrmo made heavy logging equipment.

In the early 1930s he bought a lathe and began adding machinery to his shop as the business expanded. He had few employees those first few years, and his son Arthur began working with him in 1935. In 1937 Myrmo began building logging trailers, and by the following year annual sales were $24,700 and his payroll totaled $5,200, including machinists and welders. The firm, renamed George Myrmo & Sons when Emil joined his father and brother in the business in 1938, began a small parts company because parts for the machinery they were building and selling often were not available in Eugene.

Shortly before World War II the company stopped building heavy equipment and turned to repair work instead. During the war years business was brisk as George Myrmo & Sons sold logging trailers, expanded the parts department into a major portion of the business, and repaired logging and sawmill equipment.

During the 1930s and 1940s the Myrmos had bought adjacent land to accommodate the expanding business, and by the end of the war the plant had tripled in size. George Myrmo retired after the war and his sons ran the business, which continued to thrive. By 1950 total sales had reached $569,000, and two years later another building was added to house offices and the expanded parts department.

The year 1969 was a milestone for the company. It moved to a new custom-built plant on a five-acre site in Glenwood and underwent a name change to Myrmo & Sons, Inc., to herald the arrival of another Myrmo generation into the business—Arthur's son, George. By 1975, when the firm celebrated its fiftieth anniversary, sales had reached $2.45 million, and the

Myrmos were on the verge of further expansion.

A branch was opened in Bend in 1977 to sell heavy-duty truck and industrial parts. It was expanded in 1982 to include repair work, and today both sales and service operate out of a brand new facility. In 1983 Myrmo & Sons bought land and a building in Prineville to start a satellite facility for the Bend plant.

Today Emil Myrmo is president of the corporation, Arthur is senior vice-president, George is vice-president for sales and operations, and Arthur's other son, Craig, is an outside salesman. The tiny blacksmith shop that began on the fringes of Eugene has become a multimillion-dollar corporation with multiple locations, but the family tradition that sustained it in its earliest years has never changed.

In 1969 the firm moved to a new custom-built plant on five acres in Glenwood, and adopted the present name of Myrmo & Sons, Inc.

The firm began simply as George Myrmo: Blacksmith, at this 1937 Franklin Boulevard location. The name changed to George Myrmo & Sons in 1938.

LUVAAS, COBB, RICHARDS & FRASER, P.C.

The law firm of Luvaas, Cobb, Richards & Fraser traces its roots to 1946 when John L. Luvaas, a native Eugenean with a law degree from the University of Oregon, returned home from World War II and started a general law practice. Ralph F. Cobb joined him as a partner in 1955. Two years later Joe B. Richards joined the law partnership. When Robert H. Fraser became a partner in 1966, the firm name became what it has remained for almost twenty years.

One of the oldest continuous legal firms in the city, Luvaas, Cobb, Richards & Fraser moved to its present location at 777 High Street in 1970 and has expanded its offices there over the years to accommodate a growing staff. In 1978 the firm became a professional corporation and today is a full-service law firm with seven shareholder attorneys, five associate attorneys, and a staff of eighteen.

The firm primarily handles civil litigation, with most member attorneys specializing in particular areas such as personal injury, real property, business, probate, malpractice, or domestic relations. A major area of specialization for the firm is school district work, an interest that dates back to the 1940s and early 1950s, when Luvaas served as counsel for area school districts, including Bethel, Junction City, and Pleasant Hill, as they worked toward individual consolidation. Today Luvaas, Cobb, Richards & Fraser also represents the Eugene 4-J School District, among others.

Members of the firm are active in the community, lending support in diverse areas of service. Attorneys have served on the Oregon State Bar Board of Governors and the Oregon State Bar Board of Professional Responsibility. Many are active in helping to direct numerous service organizations and state governmental agencies, including Sacred Heart Hospital, the

The shareholders and associate attorneys of Luvaas, Cobb, Richards & Fraser, P.C., are (seated, front row, left to right) Ronald A. Walro, Joe B. Richards, Ralph F. Cobb, Jaye Caroline Fraser, Thomas M. Christ, and Douglas L. McCool. In the back row (standing, left to right) are Robert L. Shaw, Robert H. Fraser, Varner J. Johns III, Dennis W. Percell (seated), Louis L. Kurtz, and John L. Luvaas.

Eugene Airport Commission, Eugene Junior Achievement, the Oregon Environmental Quality Commission, and the Oregon Water Policy Review Board.

In addition, among the firm's attorneys are four former presidents of the Lane County Bar Association, two former presidents of the Eugene Chamber of Commerce, and a former three-term representative in the Oregon Legislature. This active involvement reflects the concern of Luvaas, Cobb, Richards & Fraser for the community in which it had its beginnings—and where it plans a thriving future.

161

PATRONS

The following individuals, companies, and organizations have made a valuable commitment to the quality of this publication. Windsor Publications and the Lane County Historical Society gratefully acknowledge their participation in *Lane County: An Illustrated History of the Emerald Empire.*

Brockett Real Estate, Inc.
Janet K. Burg
Chef Francisco*
Christian Logging Co., Inc.
Clarke's Sheet Metal, Inc.*
Cone Lumber Company*
Dow Corning Corporation*
Dunham Cadillac-Oldsmobile, Inc.*
Dutch Girl Ice Cream*
Early Roofing Service, Inc.
Louis E. Epplett, D.M.D.
Eugene Moving and Storage Company*
Eugene Water & Electric Board*
First Interstate Bank of Oregon, N.A.*
The Fogelstrom Co.*
Giustina Bros.
International King's Table*
Lane Community College*
Lane County Geographical Society, Inc.
Lane County Labor Council AFL-CIO
Lochmead Farms/Dari-Mart Stores*
Luvaas, Cobb, Richards & Fraser, P.C.*
McKay Investment Company*
McKenzie-Willamette Hospital*
MAR % STAT Market Research & Analysis
Steve Moe Family - Intercity
Myrmo & Sons, Inc.*
Ethan and Lois Newman
Nike*
Northwest Natural Gas Company*
Northwest Systems*
Poole-Larsen Funeral Home and Crematorium*
RAMS Realty, Inc.
The Register-Guard*
Sacred Heart General Hospital*
Schaudt, Stemm & Wild, Inc.
Shelton-Turnbull Printers, Inc.

Skeie's Jewelers*
Hal W. Skinner, Jr.
Spectra-Physics Laser Systems Division*
Speer, Jones & Andersen, Lawyers, P.C.
Springfield Museum
The Strausbaugh Family
Stretch & Sew, Inc.*
Swanson Brothers Lumber Co., Inc.*
University of Oregon*
Wildish Group of Companies*
Willamette Poultry Co.*
The Woodard Family Foundation*
Zellner Properties*

*Partners in Progress of *Lane County: An Illustrated History of the Emerald Empire.* The histories of these companies and organizations appear in Chapter 8, beginning on page 118.

BIBLIOGRAPHY

American Institute of Architects, Southwestern Oregon Chapter. *Style and Vernacular: A Guide to the Architecture of Lane County, Oregon.* Portland, OR: Oregon Historical Society, 1983.

Barette, Leonore Gale. *Christmas in Oregon Territory in 1853.* Eugene, OR: n.p., 1950.

Beckham, Stephen Dow. *The Indians of Western Oregon.* Coos Bay, OR: Arago Books, 1977.

Beckham, Stephen Dow; Minor, Rick; and Toepel, Kathryn Anne. *Prehistory and History of BLM Lands in West-Central Oregon: A Cultural Resource Overview.* University of Oregon Anthropological Papers, no. 25. Eugene: Department of Anthropology, University of Oregon, 1981.

Berry, Don. *Trask.* New York: Viking Press, 1960.

Bowen, William A. *The Willamette Valley: Migration and Settlement on the Oregon Frontier.* Seattle: University of Washington Press, 1978.

Carey, Charles H. *General History of Oregon.* Portland: Binford & Mort, 1971.

Case, Robert Ormond. *The Empire Builders.* Portland: Binford & Mort, 1949.

Clark, Malcolm, Jr., ed. *Pharisee Among Philistines: The Diary of Judge Matthew P. Deady, 1871-1892.* Portland: Oregon Historical Society, 1975.

Clark, Robert O. *History of the Willamette Valley, Oregon.* Chicago: S.J. Clark Publishing Co., 1927.

Coons, Frederica. "The Early History of Eugene." M.A. thesis, University of Oregon, 1951.

Daniels, Roger. *Concentration Camps U.S.A.: Japanese Americans and World War II.* New York: Holt, Rinehart and Winston, 1971.

Dodds, Gordon B. *Oregon, A History.* New York: W.W. Norton & Co., 1977.

Eugene and Its Government. Eugene: League of Women Voters, 1962.

Eugene Morning Register, Anniversary Edition, 1846-1904. Held in the Oregon Collection, University of Oregon.

Fadeley, Nancie Peacocke. *Mission to Oregon.* Eugene: General Conference of the United Methodist Church, 1976.

Farmer, Judith A. *An Historical Atlas of Early Oregon.* Portland: Historical Cartographic Publications, 1973.

Ghent, W.J. *The Road to Oregon.* New York: Longman, Green & Co., 1929.

Gill, John. *Gill's Chinook Dictionary.* Portland: J.K. Gill Co., 1933.

Hewitt, James. *Eye-Witnesses to Wagon Trains West.* New York: Charles Scribner's Sons, 1973.

Historic Use of Six Reservoir Areas in the Upper Willamette Valley, Lane County, Oregon. Eugene: Heritage Research Associates, 1982.

Hunter, Wally. *The Bohemia Story.* Culp Creek, OR: Bohemia Lumber Co., 1969.

Jensen, Veryl M. *Early Days on the Upper Willamette.* Oakridge, OR: Upper Willamette Pioneer Association, 1970.

Kesey, Ken. *Sometimes a Great Notion.* New York: Viking Press, 1963.

Lane County Government Moving Forward. Eugene: Lane County Office of Community Relations, 1974.

Lockley, Fred. *Oregon Folks.* New York: Knickerbocker Press, 1927.

Loy, William. *Atlas of Oregon.* Eugene: University of Oregon Books, 1976.

Mackenzie, Cecil W. *Donald MacKenzie, King of the Northwest.* Los Angeles: Ivan Deach, Jr., 1937.

Mackey, Harold. *The Kalapuyans—A Sourcebook on the Indians of the Willamette Valley.* Salem, OR: Mission Mill Museum Association, 1974.

McArthur, Lewis. *Oregon Geographic Names.* Portland: Oregon Historical Society, 1974.

Minor, Rick, and Pecor, Audrey Frances. *Cultural Resource Overview of the Willamette National Forest, Western Oregon.* University of Oregon Anthropological Papers, no. 12. Eugene: Department of Anthropology, University of Oregon, 1977.

Moore, Lucia W.; McCornack, Nina W.; and McReady, Gladys W. *The Story of Eugene.* New York: Stratford House, 1949.

Newson, David. *The Western Observer.* Portland: Oregon Historical Society, 1972.

1970 Census; A Data Sketch of Lane County. Eugene: Lane Council of Governments, 1972.

Paulus, Norma. *Oregon Blue Book, 1983-1984.* Salem: State of Oregon, 1983.

Peterson, Pete. *Our Wagon Train Is Lost.* Eugene: New American Gothic, 1975.

Randall, J.G. *Lincoln the President.* New York: Dodd, Mead & Co., 1945.

Recreation and Tourism in Lane County. Eugene: Uniplan Associates, 1981.

Sengstacken, Agnes Ruth. *Destination West!* Portland: Binford & Mort, 1942.

Stewart, Hilary. *Indian Fishing: Early Methods on the Northwest Coast.* Seattle: University of Washington Press, 1977.

The University of Oregon: First 100 Years. Special souvenir historical issue. Eugene: Oregon Daily Emerald, 1972.

Velasco, Dorothy. *The Northwest Woman and An Evening with Thomas Condon.* Springfield, OR: Springfield Historical Commission, 1982.

Victor, Frances Fuller. *The Early Indian Wars of Oregon.* Salem: F.C. Baker, Oregon State Printer, 1894.

Walling, Albert G. *Illustrated History of Lane County, Oregon.* Portland: A.G. Walling, 1884.

Warner, Agnes Stewart. *Diary.* Transcribed and reproduced. Eugene: Lane County Historical Society, 1961.

Wayne Morse; the Record of a Working Senator in Detail. A 1968 handbook for Morse workers. Portland: Re-elect Wayne Morse Committee, 1968.

Whiteley, Opal. *The Story of Opal: The Journal of an Understanding Heart.* Boston: Atlantic Monthly Press, 1920.

Your New Lane County Government: From Sea Level to Ski Level. Eugene: Lane County Board of Commissioners, 1967.

Zucker, Jeff; Hummel, Kay; and Hogfoss, Bob. *Oregon Indians— Culture, History and Current Affairs.* Portland: Western Imprints (Oregon Historical Society), 1983.

NEWSPAPERS
Cottage Grove Sentinel
Dead Mountain Echo
Junction City Times
Oregon Daily Emerald
The Oregonian
Register-Guard
Springfield News
Siuslaw News

PERIODICALS
Lane County Historian
Oregon Historical Quarterly

INDEX

The store in Lowell was
the most important
source of provisions for
families who had settled
up the Middle Fork.
Courtesy, Lane County
Historical Museum